YOUR GUIDE TO

TO AUSTRALIA

A STEP-BY-STEP HANDBOOK

BY

WILLIAM JONES

2023

Your Guide to Moving to Australia: A Step-by-Step Handbook
By William Jones
This edition was created and published by Mamba Press
©MambaPress 2023

Contents

Preface

Australia, with its vast landscapes, unique wildlife, diverse culture, and thriving economy, has long captured the imaginations of people around the world as an ideal destination for a new beginning. Whether you're drawn to the bustling cities, pristine beaches, rugged Outback, or the promise of a better life, embarking on the journey to move to Australia is a significant decision that can be both thrilling and challenging.

This handbook, "Your Guide to Moving to Australia," has been meticulously crafted to serve as your steadfast companion on this transformative voyage. It recognizes that moving to a new country is a multifaceted experience, one that blends anticipation, uncertainty, excitement, and perhaps even a touch of anxiety. Our aim is to demystify the process, provide you with valuable insights, and offer a roadmap to navigate the intricacies of relocating to the Land Down Under.

Australia is a land of opportunity, and while the idea of starting anew here is tantalizing, it's essential to understand that it also comes with its share of complexities. From understanding the visa application process and financial planning to finding accommodation, adapting to the local culture, and building a social network, this book delves into every aspect of moving to Australia.

By taking this journey with us, you'll gain the knowledge and confidence necessary to make informed decisions at each step of the way. Whether you're an aspiring expatriate, a professional looking to advance your career, a family seeking a better quality of life, or an adventurer in search of new horizons, this guide is designed to cater to your unique needs.

As you embark on this life-changing endeavor, remember that while there may be challenges and uncertainties along the way, the rewards of living in Australia are immeasurable. With the right information, preparation, and a positive mindset, you can transform your dream of calling Australia home into a thriving reality.

We invite you to immerse yourself in the chapters that follow, absorb the knowledge, and embrace the journey. Whether your move is imminent or a distant aspiration, this guide will be your trusted resource, offering guidance, inspiration, and practical tips to ensure your transition to life in Australia is a success.

Welcome to the adventure of a lifetime, and may your story of moving to Australia be filled with joy, growth, and boundless opportunities.

- *William Jones*

Introduction

G'day mate! Welcome to the introduction of your exciting journey towards making Australia your new home. This diverse, vast, and mesmerizing country is not just a place on the map; it's an experience waiting to unfold. As you embark on the adventure of moving to Australia, you are setting out on a path filled with incredible opportunities and experiences.

Australia, often referred to as the Land Down Under, boasts a wealth of natural beauty, cultural diversity, economic prosperity, and a high quality of life. Whether you are drawn by the allure of pristine beaches, the vibrant city life, the rugged Outback, or the chance to live in a nation known for its friendly and welcoming people, you have made a choice that promises adventure, personal growth, and a future limited only by your imagination.

However, as with any significant life change, moving to Australia comes with its share of challenges and complexities. It's not just about packing your bags and boarding a plane; it's about navigating a new system, adapting to a different way of life, and building a future that aligns with your aspirations.

This book, "Your Guide to Moving to Australia," has been carefully curated to provide you with the knowledge and resources you need to navigate this transition smoothly. Whether you are a skilled professional seeking career advancement, a family looking to provide a better life for your loved ones, an adventurer chasing new horizons, or anyone with a dream of calling Australia home, this guide is tailored to your unique journey.

Each chapter is a step-by-step guide that addresses critical aspects of your move, from understanding Australian visas and managing your finances to finding accommodation, integrating into the local culture, and thriving in your new environment. Whether you're in the early stages of considering the move or already in the thick of the process, this handbook will serve as your dependable companion.

As you turn the pages, you'll gain insights into the intricacies of Australian life, discover valuable tips and advice from seasoned expatriates, and find resources to make informed decisions every step of the way.

Moving to Australia is not just about changing your address; it's about embracing a new way of life and immersing yourself in a land of opportunities. With the right guidance, preparation, and a positive outlook, you can transform your dream into a thriving reality.

So, dear reader, take a deep breath, set aside any apprehensions, and prepare to embark on a journey that will shape your future in extraordinary ways. Australia is waiting to welcome you with open arms, and this book is here to guide you on your path to a new beginning.

Get ready to make your dreams come true in the Land Down Under!

- William Jones

The Decision to Move

Making the decision to move to another country is a profound step that often begins with a sense of restlessness and a yearning for change. It's a choice that can transform your life in countless ways, and it's not to be taken lightly. In this chapter, we will explore the various factors and considerations that play a pivotal role in the decision-making process when it comes to moving to Australia.

The allure of Australia is undeniable. With its stunning natural landscapes, rich cultural tapestry, thriving job market, and renowned quality of life, it's no wonder that countless individuals and families from around the world are drawn to this continent-sized nation. Yet, before you pack your bags and embark on this life-changing adventure, there are important questions to ponder and critical decisions to make.

The Catalyst for Change

Many people contemplate the idea of moving to Australia because they are seeking change in their lives. It could be change on various fronts - career, lifestyle, environment, or personal development. Identifying the catalyst for this change is a fundamental starting point.

Career Advancement: Australia has a robust economy and offers a wide range of job opportunities in various sectors. If you're looking to further your career or enter a new field, Australia's thriving job market may be the motivation behind your move.

Quality of Life: Australia consistently ranks high in global quality of life indices. If you're seeking a better quality of life with access to excellent healthcare, education, and a work-life balance that allows for leisure and family time, Australia could be your ideal destination.

Adventure and Exploration: The allure of adventure, exploration, and experiencing a new culture can be a compelling reason to move. Australia's diverse landscapes, wildlife, and vibrant cities offer endless opportunities for exploration.

Family Considerations: For some, the decision to move is driven by family considerations. This may include reuniting with family members already living in Australia, providing a better future for your children, or seeking a safer and more secure environment.

Educational Opportunities: Australia is home to world-class universities and educational institutions. If you're looking to pursue higher education or provide your children with top-notch schooling, this may be a significant factor in your decision.

Weighing the Pros and Cons

Once you've identified your motivation for moving to Australia, it's essential to conduct a comprehensive analysis of the potential pros and cons. This step is critical as it allows you to make an informed decision based on your individual circumstances and priorities.

Pros of Moving to Australia

1. **Economic Opportunities**: Australia's strong economy provides ample job opportunities, competitive salaries, and a high standard of living.
2. **Healthcare**: The country boasts an excellent healthcare system, including universal healthcare for permanent residents.
3. **Education**: Australia offers a world-class education system, from primary to tertiary levels.
4. **Cultural Diversity**: Australia is a melting pot of cultures, offering a rich tapestry of traditions, cuisines, and experiences.
5. **Natural Beauty**: From the Great Barrier Reef to the Outback, Australia's natural landscapes are breathtaking and provide opportunities for adventure and exploration.
6. **Safety and Security**: Australia is known for its safety and political stability, making it an attractive destination for families.

Cons of Moving to Australia

1. **Distance from Home**: Australia is often far from many countries, resulting in long flights and limited opportunities for frequent visits home.
2. **Cost of Living**: While salaries are competitive, the cost of living, particularly in major cities like Sydney and Melbourne, can be high.
3. **Cultural Adjustment**: Adjusting to a new culture and way of life can be challenging, and some individuals may experience culture shock.
4. **Immigration Process**: Navigating the immigration process can be complex and time-consuming.
5. **Isolation**: Depending on your location, you may experience a sense of isolation due to Australia's vast geography.
6. **Climate**: Australia's climate can be extreme, with hot summers, cold winters, and regions prone to bushfires and floods.

Setting Clear Goals

As you weigh the pros and cons of moving to Australia, it's crucial to set clear and realistic goals for your relocation. What do you hope to achieve by making this move, and what are your expectations? Here are some key considerations:

1. **Short-Term vs. Long-Term**: Are you planning to stay in Australia temporarily for a specific project or adventure, or is this a long-term commitment?
2. **Career Goals**: If career advancement is your primary motivation, what specific career goals do you aim to achieve in Australia?
3. **Lifestyle Objectives**: What kind of lifestyle do you envision in Australia? How will it differ from your current lifestyle?

4. **Family Planning**: If you have a family, how will the move impact your spouse and children? What are their goals and expectations?

5. **Financial Planning**: What financial preparations do you need to make before and after the move?

6. **Personal Growth**: How do you anticipate personal growth and development in Australia?

Setting clear goals will provide you with a roadmap for your journey and help you make informed decisions along the way. It's important to remember that the decision to move to Australia is a significant one, and there is no one-size-fits-all approach. Your goals and priorities will shape your unique experience.

In the chapters that follow, we will delve deeper into the practical aspects of moving to Australia, including visa options, financial planning, finding accommodation, and navigating the intricacies of Australian society. This book is designed to be your comprehensive guide, providing you with the knowledge and resources you need to turn your decision to move to Australia into a well-planned and successful reality.

Understanding Australian Visas

Australia's immigration system is known for its complexity, but it's also renowned for offering a wide array of visa options tailored to various needs and circumstances. Navigating the visa landscape is a crucial step on your journey to move to Australia. In this chapter, we will explore the different types of Australian visas, their eligibility criteria, and the application process.

The Visa System

Australia's visa system is designed to cater to a diverse range of individuals, from skilled workers and students to family members and refugees. The type of visa you need depends on your specific situation and the purpose of your move to Australia. Let's delve into some of the most common visa categories:

1. **Temporary Work Visas**

a. Temporary Skill Shortage (TSS) Visa (Subclass 482): This visa is for skilled workers sponsored by an Australian employer. It allows you to work in Australia temporarily and may lead to permanent residency.

b. Working Holiday Visa (Subclass 417 and 462): These visas are for young adults (typically aged 18-30) from eligible countries who want to work and travel in Australia for up to 12 months.

2. **Permanent Work Visas**

a. Employer Nomination Scheme (ENS) Visa (Subclass 186): This visa allows skilled workers nominated by their employer to work and live in Australia permanently.

b. Skilled Independent Visa (Subclass 189): This points-tested visa is for skilled workers who are not sponsored by an employer or family member. It leads to permanent residency.

c. Skilled Nominated Visa (Subclass 190): This state-nominated visa is for skilled workers who have been nominated by an Australian state or territory government.

3. **Student Visas**

a. Student Visa (Subclass 500): This visa is for international students who want to study in Australia. It allows you to work part-time while studying and provides opportunities for post-study work.

4. **Family Visas**

a. Partner Visa (Subclass 820/801 or 309/100): These visas are for partners of Australian citizens, permanent residents, or eligible New Zealand citizens.

b. Parent Visa (Subclass 103): This visa allows parents of Australian citizens, permanent residents, or eligible New Zealand citizens to live in Australia.

5. **Refugee and Humanitarian Visas**

a. Protection Visa (Subclass 866): This visa is for people seeking protection in Australia due to fear of persecution in their home country.

b. Global Special Humanitarian Visa (Subclass 202): This visa is for individuals who are subject to substantial discrimination or human rights abuses in their home country.

6. **Visitor Visas**

a. Visitor Visa (Subclass 600): This visa allows you to visit Australia for tourism, business meetings, or to visit family and friends.

It's important to note that this is not an exhaustive list, and the Australian government may introduce new visa categories or change existing ones. Therefore, it's crucial to check the official Australian Department of Home Affairs website for the most up-to-date information on visa options.

Eligibility Criteria

Each visa category has specific eligibility criteria, and meeting these criteria is essential for a successful visa application. The eligibility requirements can vary widely, but here are some common factors considered for many visas:

1. **Age**: Some visas, such as working holiday visas, have age restrictions.
2. **Skills and Qualifications**: Skilled worker visas require specific skills and qualifications relevant to the nominated occupation.
3. **Health and Character**: Applicants must meet health and character requirements, which typically involve medical examinations and police checks.
4. **Sponsorship**: Some visas, like the employer-sponsored visas, require sponsorship from an eligible Australian employer.
5. **English Language Proficiency**: Certain visas may require proof of English language proficiency, often through standardized tests like IELTS.
6. **Financial Capacity**: Applicants may need to demonstrate their ability to support themselves and their dependents while in Australia.
7. **Family Relationships**: Family visas are typically granted based on the relationship between the applicant and the sponsoring family member.
8. **Refugee Status**: Refugee and humanitarian visas are granted based on the applicant's status as a refugee or their need for humanitarian protection.

The Application Process

Navigating the visa application process can be complex, and it's advisable to seek professional advice or assistance, especially for more complicated visa categories. However, here is a simplified overview of the general application process:

1. **Select the Right Visa**: Carefully review the available visa options and select the one that best matches your circumstances and goals.
2. **Check Eligibility**: Thoroughly read the eligibility criteria for

your chosen visa to ensure you meet all requirements.

3. **Gather Documents**: Collect all necessary documents, including identity documents, educational qualifications, employment records, and health and character assessments.

4. **Create an ImmiAccount**: ImmiAccount is the online platform where you submit your visa application. Create an account on the official Australian Department of Home Affairs website.

5. **Complete the Application Form**: Fill out the visa application form accurately and provide all requested information.

6. **Pay the Visa Fee**: Pay the application fee, which varies depending on the visa type.

7. **Submit Your Application**: Upload all required documents and submit your application through your ImmiAccount.

8. **Biometrics and Health Checks**: If necessary, attend biometric appointments and complete health checks as specified by the visa requirements.

9. **Wait for Processing**: Visa processing times can vary, so be prepared for a waiting period. You can check the progress of your application through your ImmiAccount.

10. **Visa Grant or Refusal**: If your application is approved, you will receive a visa grant notification. If it's refused, you will be informed of the reasons for the refusal.

11. **Plan Your Move**: Once your visa is granted, start planning your move to Australia, including travel arrangements, accommodation, and any other logistics.

12. **Comply with Visa Conditions**: Ensure you understand and comply with the conditions of your visa, including any work, study, or residency requirements.

Professional Guidance

While it's possible to navigate the visa application process independently, seeking professional guidance can significantly enhance your chances of success, particularly for more complex visa categories. Migration agents and lawyers specialize in immigration law and can provide expert advice, assist with document preparation, and represent you during the application process.

Before engaging a migration agent or lawyer, ensure they are registered with the Office of the Migration Agents Registration Authority (MARA) if they are operating in Australia. If you're applying for a visa from outside Australia, check for reputable professionals with expertise in Australian immigration law.

Understanding the Australian visa system is a crucial step in your journey to make Australia your new home. By carefully assessing your eligibility, selecting the right visa, and following the application process diligently, you can pave the way for a successful move to this vibrant and welcoming country. In the chapters that follow, we will delve deeper into the practical aspects of preparing for your move, including financial planning, finding accommodation, and settling into Australian society.

Planning Your Finances

Moving to Australia is a significant step, both personally and financially. Proper financial planning is essential to ensure a smooth transition and a secure future in your new homeland. In this chapter, we will explore the key aspects of planning your finances when moving to Australia, from budgeting for your move to managing currency exchange and understanding the Australian financial system.

Budgeting for Your Move

Before you set foot on Australian soil, it's crucial to establish a clear financial plan that covers all aspects of your move. Moving costs can quickly add up, so a well-thought-out budget is your best ally in managing expenses.

1. **Initial Expenses**

- **Visa Application Fees**: Calculate the fees associated with your visa application, which can vary depending on the type of visa you're applying for.
- **Travel Expenses**: Include the cost of airfare, transportation to your destination city, and accommodation for your initial stay.
- **Health Insurance**: Budget for health insurance premiums, especially if you are not eligible for Medicare (Australia's public healthcare system).
- **Temporary Accommodation**: If you plan to stay in temporary accommodation while searching for permanent housing, allocate funds for rent and security deposits.
- **Settling-In Costs**: Plan for initial expenses such as groceries, household items, and transportation within Australia.

2. **Living Expenses**

- **Housing Costs**: Estimate your monthly rent or mortgage payments, including utilities, property taxes, and maintenance.
- **Transportation**: Budget for public transportation, car expenses (if applicable), and fuel costs.
- **Groceries and Dining**: Allocate funds for groceries, dining out, and entertainment.
- **Healthcare**: Include health insurance premiums and out-of-pocket medical expenses.
- **Education**: If you have school-age children, budget for education expenses such as school fees and uniforms.
- **Emergency Fund**: It's wise to set aside some money as an emergency fund to cover unexpected expenses.

3. Currency Exchange

Moving to Australia likely involves dealing with different currencies, and currency exchange rates can impact the value of your money. Here are some tips for managing currency exchange:

- **Exchange Rates**: Keep an eye on exchange rates and consider exchanging currency when rates are favorable.
- **Bank Accounts**: Open an Australian bank account as soon as possible to avoid excessive currency conversion fees. Many banks offer currency exchange services with competitive rates.
- **Transfer Services**: Compare international money transfer services to find the most cost-effective option for transferring your funds to Australia.
- **Hedging Strategies**: For larger sums of money, consider hedging strategies to protect against unfavorable exchange rate movements.

Australian Banking System

Understanding the Australian banking system is crucial for managing your finances effectively during your stay in the country. Here are some key points to consider:

1. **Types of Banks**

- **Major Banks**: Australia has several major banks, including Commonwealth Bank, Westpac, ANZ, and National Australia Bank (NAB). These banks offer a wide range of services and have extensive branch networks.
- **Smaller Banks**: There are also smaller banks, credit unions, and building societies that may offer competitive products and services.
- **Online Banks**: Online-only banks are becoming increasingly popular in Australia, offering lower fees and higher interest rates on savings accounts.

2. **Bank Accounts**

- **Everyday Transaction Accounts**: These accounts are used for everyday spending and typically come with a debit card.
- **Savings Accounts**: Savings accounts offer higher interest rates but may have restrictions on withdrawals.
- **Term Deposits**: Term deposits provide fixed interest rates for a specific period, usually ranging from a few months to several years.
- **Foreign Currency Accounts**: Some banks offer foreign currency accounts, which can be useful for managing funds in multiple currencies.

3. **Credit Cards**

- **Credit Cards**: Australian banks offer a variety of credit cards with different features, including rewards programs and low-interest options. Be mindful of interest rates and fees.
- **Credit Score**: Establishing a good credit history in Australia can be important for future financial transactions, such as obtaining a mortgage.

4. Mortgages and Loans

- **Home Loans**: If you plan to buy property in Australia, research the mortgage market and get pre-approval for a home loan.
- **Personal Loans**: Personal loans are available for various purposes, such as car purchases or home improvements.

5. Investment Options

- **Savings and Term Deposits**: These are low-risk, interest-bearing investment options offered by banks.
- **Shares and Managed Funds**: Consider exploring the Australian stock market and managed funds for potential investments.
- **Property**: Real estate can be a popular investment choice in Australia, but it requires careful research and financial planning.

6. Taxation

- **Tax File Number (TFN)**: Obtain a TFN, a unique identifier for taxation purposes in Australia. You can apply for a TFN online.
- **Income Tax**: Australia has a progressive income tax system,

and your tax obligations will depend on your income and residency status.

- **Superannuation**: Learn about the Australian superannuation system, which is a mandatory retirement savings scheme. Employers are required to contribute a portion of your salary to your superannuation account.

7. Financial Advisors

- **Professional Advice**: Consider seeking the advice of a financial advisor or planner with expertise in Australian financial regulations and taxation.
- **Visa-Specific Advice**: Some visa categories may have specific financial requirements. Consult with experts who specialize in your visa type if necessary.

Building a Financial Safety Net

Moving to a new country involves uncertainties and adjustments. Building a financial safety net can provide peace of mind during this transitional period. Here are some strategies:

1. **Emergency Fund**: Maintain an emergency fund equivalent to at least three to six months of living expenses to cover unexpected costs like medical bills or job loss.
2. **Health Insurance**: Ensure you have appropriate health insurance coverage to mitigate the financial impact of medical expenses.
3. **Income Protection**: Consider income protection insurance to safeguard your income in case you are unable to work due to illness or injury.
4. **Debt Management**: Manage any existing debts responsibly and have a plan for paying them down.

5. **Financial Goals**: Set clear financial goals and regularly review your progress to stay on track.

Seeking Professional Advice

If you find the Australian financial system complex or have unique financial circumstances, consider consulting a financial advisor or planner. They can help you navigate tax regulations, investment options, and retirement planning specific to your situation. Additionally, they can provide guidance on optimizing your financial strategy while living in Australia.

Planning your finances is a critical component of your successful transition to life in Australia. By budgeting wisely, managing currency exchange effectively, and understanding the Australian banking and taxation systems, you can lay a strong financial foundation for your new adventure. In the chapters that follow, we will delve into other essential aspects of moving to Australia, including finding accommodation, healthcare, and education options.

Finding Accommodation

Securing suitable accommodation is a pivotal step in settling into your new life in Australia. The type of housing you choose, its location, and its affordability can significantly impact your overall living experience. In this chapter, we will explore the various aspects of finding accommodation in Australia, whether you're seeking a rental property or considering purchasing a home.

Rental Accommodation

Renting is a common choice for newcomers to Australia, offering flexibility and the ability to explore different neighborhoods before committing to a long-term location. Here's what you need to know about finding rental accommodation in Australia:

1. **Research and Planning**

- **Location**: Determine the areas or suburbs where you'd like to live. Consider factors like proximity to work, public transportation, schools, and amenities.
- **Budget**: Set a realistic budget for your rental expenses, including rent, utilities, and potential bond (security deposit).
- **Property Type**: Decide on the type of property you need, such as apartments, houses, townhouses, or shared accommodations.

2. **Property Search**

- **Online Listings**: Websites like realestate.com.au, domain.com.au, and flatmates.com.au are valuable resources for searching available properties.
- **Real Estate Agents**: Many rental properties are managed by real estate agents. You can contact local agencies to inquire

about their listings.

- **Newspaper Listings**: Some rental properties are advertised in local newspapers.
- **Networking**: Utilize your social and professional networks to seek recommendations for available properties.

3. Property Inspection

- **Schedule Visits**: Arrange to visit potential rental properties to assess their condition, location, and suitability.
- **Inspect Carefully**: During inspections, check for issues like maintenance problems, pests, and the overall condition of the property.
- **Ask Questions**: Don't hesitate to ask the property manager or landlord questions about the property, lease terms, and included amenities.

4. Application Process

- **Application Form**: Complete a rental application form, which typically includes personal information, rental history, and references.
- **References**: Provide references from previous landlords or property managers to strengthen your application.
- **Proof of Income**: Demonstrate your ability to pay rent by providing proof of income, such as pay stubs or employment contracts.
- **Bond**: Be prepared to pay a bond, usually equivalent to several weeks' rent, as a security deposit. This amount is refundable when you leave the property if there is no damage or unpaid rent.

5. Lease Agreement

- **Read Carefully**: Review the lease agreement carefully before signing. Pay attention to the lease term, rent amount, and any special conditions.
- **Tenant Rights**: Familiarize yourself with your rights and responsibilities as a tenant in Australia. Each state or territory may have specific tenancy laws.
- **Insurance**: Consider tenant's insurance to protect your belongings in case of theft or damage.

6. Utilities

- **Connection**: Arrange for utility connections such as electricity, gas, water, and internet services. Some rental properties may include utilities in the rent.
- **Billing**: Understand how utility bills are calculated and when they are due.

Buying Property

If you're considering purchasing a home in Australia, you'll need to navigate the property market and mortgage options. Here's what you should know:

1. Property Market

- **Research**: Investigate the property market in your desired location. Look at property prices, trends, and potential growth areas.
- **Property Inspection**: Attend open houses and inspections to get a feel for the properties available.

2. Financing

- **Mortgage Pre-Approval**: Before you start house hunting, obtain pre-approval for a mortgage. This helps you understand your budget and makes you a more attractive buyer.
- **Deposit**: Save for a deposit, typically around 10% of the property's purchase price.
- **Mortgage Broker**: Consider using a mortgage broker to help you find the most suitable loan and navigate the application process.

3. Property Purchase

- **Negotiation**: Once you find a property you like, negotiate the purchase price with the seller or their agent.
- **Contract of Sale**: Review the contract of sale and seek legal advice if needed.
- **Property Inspection**: Conduct a thorough property inspection, including building and pest inspections if required.
- **Conveyancing**: Engage a conveyancer or solicitor to handle the legal aspects of the property transfer.
- **Settlement**: Complete the purchase at settlement, where the property officially changes ownership.

4. Additional Costs

- **Stamp Duty**: Be aware of stamp duty, a tax imposed on property purchases. Rates vary by state or territory.
- **Legal and Conveyancing Fees**: Budget for legal and conveyancing fees associated with the property purchase.
- **Insurance**: Consider home and contents insurance to protect your investment.

- **Utilities**: Arrange for utility connections and understand ongoing costs.

5. Home Ownership

- **Strata Properties**: If you purchase a unit or apartment, you may be part of a strata scheme, which involves shared maintenance costs and rules.
- **Property Maintenance**: Plan for ongoing property maintenance, repairs, and renovations as needed.
- **Council Rates**: Budget for council rates, which fund local government services.
- **Home Loans**: Continue making mortgage payments according to your loan agreement.

Shared Accommodation

If you're looking for cost-effective accommodation options or prefer a shared living arrangement, shared housing or flatmates can be a suitable choice. Here are some considerations:

- **Online Platforms**: Websites like flatmates.com.au and gumtree.com.au allow you to search for available shared accommodations and potential flatmates.
- **Compatibility**: When sharing with others, consider compatibility in terms of lifestyle, habits, and expectations.
- **Lease Agreements**: Ensure that lease agreements and shared expenses are clear and agreed upon in writing.
- **Legal Considerations**: Be aware of your rights and responsibilities as a tenant or housemate in shared accommodation.

Temporary Accommodation

If you haven't secured permanent accommodation upon your arrival in Australia, temporary housing options can provide a comfortable transition:

- **Hotels**: Stay in a hotel or serviced apartment for a short period while you search for a permanent place.
- **Short-Term Rentals**: Platforms like Airbnb offer short-term rentals and furnished apartments that can serve as temporary accommodations.
- **Hostels and Backpackers**: Hostels and backpacker accommodations are budget-friendly options, particularly for solo travelers.

Summary

Finding accommodation in Australia requires careful planning and consideration. Whether you choose to rent, buy, or share housing, it's essential to research your options, understand your budget, and be aware of your rights and responsibilities as a tenant or property owner. Accommodation plays a significant role in your overall experience in Australia, so take the time to find the right fit for your lifestyle and needs.

In the chapters that follow, we will continue to explore essential aspects of your move to Australia, including healthcare, education options, and employment prospects.

Healthcare and Insurance

Access to quality healthcare is a fundamental aspect of your well-being when moving to Australia. Fortunately, Australia offers a world-class healthcare system that ensures residents have access to essential medical services. In this chapter, we will delve into the Australian healthcare system, the importance of health insurance, and how to navigate the healthcare landscape.

The Australian Healthcare System

Australia's healthcare system, known as Medicare, is a universal, publicly funded system that provides essential medical services to Australian citizens and permanent residents. Here are key features of the Australian healthcare system:

- **Medicare**: Medicare covers a range of medical services, including doctor visits, hospital care, and some prescription medications. It is funded through the Medicare Levy, which is a tax on eligible individuals' income.
- **Bulk Billing**: Many healthcare providers offer bulk billing, which means they bill Medicare directly for the services they provide, leaving you with little or no out-of-pocket expenses.
- **Private Health Insurance**: While Medicare provides a basic level of coverage, many Australians also opt for private health insurance to access additional services and reduce wait times for elective procedures.
- **Pharmaceutical Benefits Scheme (PBS)**: The PBS subsidizes the cost of prescription medications, making them more affordable for residents.
- **Primary Care**: General practitioners (GPs) serve as the first point of contact for most healthcare needs. You can choose your own GP, and their services are covered by Medicare.

- **Hospitals**: Public hospitals in Australia provide emergency and essential medical care. Elective surgeries and non-emergency treatments may have waiting lists in the public system.

Medicare Eligibility

As a newcomer to Australia, your eligibility for Medicare depends on your visa status:

- **Permanent Residents and Citizens**: Australian citizens and permanent residents are eligible for full Medicare benefits.
- **Temporary Residents**: Some temporary visa holders are eligible for Medicare services, primarily those from countries with reciprocal healthcare agreements. These agreements cover essential medical care but may not include all services. It's essential to check your eligibility before relying solely on Medicare.

Health Insurance in Australia

While Medicare provides essential healthcare coverage, many residents choose to supplement it with private health insurance. Here's why private health insurance is worth considering:

1. Choice and Flexibility

- **Choice of Provider**: Private health insurance allows you to choose your healthcare provider, including specialists and hospitals.
- **Timely Care**: Private health insurance can reduce waiting times for elective surgeries and specialist appointments.

2. Covering Extras

- **Extras Cover**: Private health insurance often includes extras cover for services like dental, optical, physiotherapy, and chiropractic care.
- **Hospital Cover**: Hospital cover can provide access to private hospitals and your choice of doctor for in-patient treatment.

3. Avoiding Medicare Levy Surcharge (MLS)

- **Income Threshold**: If your income exceeds a certain threshold and you do not have eligible private health insurance, you may be subject to the MLS, an additional tax on top of the Medicare Levy.
- **Reducing MLS**: Having eligible private health insurance can exempt you from the MLS or reduce the surcharge rate.

4. Lifetime Health Cover (LHC)

- **Incentive for Early Enrollment**: LHC is designed to encourage people to take out private health insurance earlier in life. If you delay taking out private health insurance, you may pay a higher premium when you eventually do.

Types of Health Insurance

Australia offers various types of private health insurance policies to cater to different needs and budgets:

1. Hospital Cover

- **Basic**: Covers essential hospital treatments, such as accommodation and medical fees in private hospitals for a restricted range of services.
- **Medium**: Provides more comprehensive coverage for a broader range of treatments and services.
- **Top**: Offers the highest level of coverage, including access to

a wide range of treatments and services in private hospitals.

2. Extras Cover

- **General**: Covers services like dental, optical, and physiotherapy.
- **Major**: Includes additional services like orthodontics and hearing aids.

3. Combined Policies

- **Hospital and Extras**: Combines hospital and extras cover into a single policy for comprehensive coverage.

4. Ambulance Cover

- Ambulance cover is often a separate policy or included as an optional extra in private health insurance.

Health Insurance Waiting Periods

When you take out private health insurance, be aware of waiting periods:

- **General Waiting Period**: A waiting period usually applies when you first take out a policy. It can range from 2 to 12 months, depending on the service or condition.
- **Pre-Existing Conditions**: If you have a pre-existing condition, insurers may impose a waiting period before you can claim benefits related to that condition.
- **Waiting Period Waivers**: In some cases, insurers may waive waiting periods for services like accidents or newborns.

Choosing a Health Insurance Provider

When selecting a health insurance provider in Australia, consider the following factors:

- **Coverage**: Evaluate the range of services and treatments covered by the policy, including any exclusions.
- **Premiums**: Compare premium costs and understand any annual increases.
- **Choice of Providers**: Check if the policy allows you to choose your healthcare providers and hospitals.
- **Extras**: If extras cover is important to you, review the benefits and limits for services like dental and physiotherapy.
- **Customer Service**: Assess the insurer's reputation for customer service and claims processing.
- **Excess and Co-Payments**: Understand any excess or co-payment requirements for hospital admissions.

Applying for Private Health Insurance

Applying for private health insurance in Australia is straightforward:

1. **Compare Policies**: Use online comparison tools or consult with insurance brokers to compare policies from different providers.
2. **Choose a Policy**: Select a policy that meets your needs and budget.
3. **Apply**: Complete the insurer's application form and provide the necessary personal and contact information.
4. **Waiting Period**: Be mindful of any waiting periods associated with your chosen policy.
5. **Payment**: Set up the payment method for your premiums, which can be monthly, quarterly, or annually.
6. **Policy Documents**: Review the policy documents carefully

to understand your coverage and any terms and conditions.

Health Services in Australia

Australia offers a comprehensive range of health services and providers, including:

- **General Practitioners (GPs)**: These primary care doctors are often your first point of contact for medical concerns. You can choose your own GP, and their services are typically bulk-billed.
- **Specialists**: Access to specialists usually requires a referral from a GP. Private health insurance can provide more choice in selecting specialists.
- **Hospitals**: Public hospitals provide emergency care and essential medical services. Private health insurance may grant access to private hospitals and shorter wait times for elective procedures.
- **Dental Care**: Dental care is not fully covered by Medicare. Consider extras cover in private health insurance for dental services.
- **Pharmacies**: Pharmacies are readily available, and prescription medications are subsidized through the Pharmaceutical Benefits Scheme (PBS).
- **Mental Health Services**: Australia has a strong focus on mental health, with a range of services available.

Staying Healthy

Maintaining good health is essential when living in Australia. Here are some tips for staying healthy:

- **Regular Check-Ups**: Schedule regular check-ups with your GP to monitor your health.

- **Vaccinations**: Stay up to date with recommended vaccinations and immunizations.
- **Healthy Lifestyle**: Maintain a balanced diet, engage in regular physical activity, and manage stress.
- **Health Education**: Educate yourself about healthcare services and conditions relevant to your age and lifestyle.
- **Mental Health**: Pay attention to your mental health and seek help if needed.

Emergency Healthcare

In case of a medical emergency, call 000 for immediate assistance. Emergency services in Australia are highly responsive and well-equipped to handle a wide range of medical situations.

Summary

Understanding the Australian healthcare system and having the right health insurance coverage are crucial aspects of your move to Australia. While Medicare provides essential coverage, private health insurance can offer additional benefits and choice. Taking the time to research and select the right insurance policy for your needs and budget is a wise investment in your health and well-being.

In the chapters that follow, we will continue to explore essential aspects of your move to Australia, including education options, employment prospects, and adapting to Australian society.

Education and Childcare

Choosing the right education and childcare options for your family is a significant consideration when moving to Australia. The country offers a diverse range of educational institutions, from primary schools to world-renowned universities, as well as various childcare services to support working parents. In this chapter, we will explore the Australian education system, childcare options, and the steps to ensure your child's educational success in this new environment.

The Australian Education System

Australia boasts a robust and internationally recognized education system that welcomes students of all ages, backgrounds, and nationalities. Understanding the structure and key features of the Australian education system is essential for making informed decisions about your child's education.

1. Early Childhood Education and Care

- **Preschool**: Children aged 3 to 5 typically attend preschool or kindergarten to develop essential social and cognitive skills.
- **Childcare Centers**: Childcare centers provide full-day care and early education programs for infants and toddlers.

2. Primary Education

- **Primary Schools**: Primary education begins at age 5 or 6 and typically covers grades K-6. The curriculum focuses on core subjects like English, mathematics, science, and social studies.
- **Curriculum**: Australian primary schools follow the national curriculum, which is consistent across the country and emphasizes literacy and numeracy skills.

3. Secondary Education

- **High Schools**: High school education spans grades 7-12. The curriculum broadens to include a wider range of subjects, and students prepare for further education or the workforce.
- **Senior Secondary Certificate**: In the final years of high school (grades 11 and 12), students work towards achieving the Senior Secondary Certificate of Education (SSCE), often referred to as the Year 12 certificate.

4. Post-Secondary Education

- **Tertiary Education**: After completing high school, students can pursue tertiary education at universities, technical and further education (TAFE) colleges, or vocational education and training (VET) institutions.
- **Bachelor's Degrees**: Universities offer bachelor's degree programs that typically span three to four years.
- **Vocational Courses**: TAFE colleges and VET institutions provide hands-on, job-focused training in various fields.
- **Higher Education**: Australia's universities are renowned for their quality and diversity of programs. Many international students choose Australia for higher education.

5. Education Pathways

- **Transition**: Students can transition from one level of education to another, and the Australian Qualifications Framework (AQF) facilitates the recognition of qualifications.
- **University Pathways**: Successful completion of Year 12 or an equivalent qualification (e.g., the International Baccalaureate)

is usually required for university admission.

- **TAFE and VET**: TAFE and VET courses offer pathways to university or direct entry into the workforce, depending on the program.

Schooling Options

Australia provides a variety of schooling options to cater to different needs and preferences:

1. Government Schools

- **Publicly Funded**: Government schools, also known as public schools, are funded by state and territory governments, making them accessible to residents at little or no cost.
- **Quality Education**: Government schools offer quality education and follow the national curriculum.

2. Catholic and Independent Schools

- **Private Institutions**: Catholic and independent schools are privately funded and may charge tuition fees.
- **Diverse Curriculum**: These schools often provide a diverse range of extracurricular activities and offer specialized programs.

3. Specialized Schools

- **Language Schools**: Some schools offer language immersion programs to help students become proficient in languages other than English.
- **Special Education**: Special education schools cater to students with specific learning needs or disabilities.

4. International Schools

- **International Curriculum**: International schools follow foreign curricula, such as the International Baccalaureate (IB) or the curriculum of another country.
- **Diverse Student Body**: These schools often have a culturally diverse student population, making them suitable for expatriate families.

Enrolling Your Child in School

Enrolling your child in an Australian school is a straightforward process:

1. **Residency Status**: Ensure that you and your child have the appropriate visa and residency status to access Australian schools.
2. **Locate Schools**: Research and identify suitable schools in your area or desired location.
3. **Contact Schools**: Contact the chosen schools to inquire about enrollment requirements, application deadlines, and availability.
4. **Documentation**: Prepare the necessary documentation, which may include proof of residence, identification, and immunization records.
5. **Application**: Complete the school's enrollment application form and submit it along with the required documents.
6. **Orientation**: Attend orientation sessions or interviews as required by the school.

Childcare and Early Learning

Australia offers various childcare and early learning options to support working parents and promote early childhood development:

1. Long Day Care

- **Full-Day Care**: Long day care centers provide full-day care and early education for children from infancy to preschool age.
- **Structured Curriculum**: These centers follow a structured curriculum that includes educational activities and play.

2. Family Day Care

- **Home-Based Care**: Family day care involves care provided by registered educators in their homes.
- **Small Groups**: Children in family day care are often in small groups, which can offer a more personalized experience.

3. Preschool and Kindergarten

- **Pre-Kindergarten Programs**: Preschool and kindergarten programs are designed for children aged 3 to 5 and focus on preparing them for primary school.
- **Developmental Milestones**: These programs help children develop social, cognitive, and emotional skills.

4. Outside School Hours Care (OSHC)

- **Before and After School Care**: OSHC services cater to school-aged children by providing care before and after school.
- **Vacation Care**: Some OSHC programs also offer vacation care during school holidays.

5. Nannies and Au Pairs

- **In-Home Care**: Families may choose to hire nannies or au pairs to provide in-home childcare services.

- **Flexible Scheduling**: In-home care can offer more flexibility in terms of hours and care arrangements.

Childcare Subsidies

The Australian government provides financial assistance to eligible families to help cover the cost of childcare:

- **Child Care Subsidy (CCS)**: CCS is means-tested and helps reduce childcare fees for eligible families. The subsidy amount depends on factors such as family income and the type of care used.
- **Additional Child Care Subsidy (ACCS)**: ACCS provides extra assistance to families facing unique or challenging circumstances, such as grandparents providing care or families in crisis.

Supporting Your Child's Education

Ensuring your child's educational success in Australia involves several key strategies:

1. **Engage with the School**: Stay actively involved in your child's education by attending parent-teacher meetings, school events, and volunteering opportunities.
2. **Support Homework and Study**: Create a conducive environment for homework and study, and provide encouragement and guidance when needed.
3. **Encourage Extracurricular Activities**: Encourage your child to participate in extracurricular activities, such as sports, arts, and clubs, to develop their interests and skills.
4. **Promote Multilingualism**: If your child speaks another language at home, maintain their proficiency and cultural connections.

5. **Address Learning Challenges**: If your child faces learning challenges, seek assistance from teachers, counselors, or specialists to provide appropriate support.

Education for International Students

If you are an international student or your child is, you can explore various options for studying in Australia:

- **Student Visas**: Apply for a student visa to pursue primary, secondary, or tertiary education in Australia.
- **English Language Courses**: Australia is a popular destination for English language courses and exam preparation, such as IELTS and TOEFL.
- **International Baccalaureate (IB)**: Consider the IB program, which is offered in many Australian schools and recognized worldwide.

Summary

Navigating the Australian education system and choosing the right childcare and school for your child is a critical aspect of your move to Australia. With a diverse range of educational institutions, flexible childcare options, and government support programs, Australia provides an excellent environment for your child's development and educational success.

In the chapters that follow, we will continue to explore essential aspects of your move to Australia, including employment opportunities, cultural integration, and practical tips for settling into your new home.

Employment and Job Search

Finding employment is a crucial aspect of your relocation to Australia. The country offers a dynamic job market with diverse opportunities across various industries. In this chapter, we will guide you through the process of seeking employment in Australia, including job search strategies, preparing your job application, and understanding the Australian workplace culture.

The Australian Job Market

Australia's economy is characterized by its stability, robustness, and diverse range of industries. Understanding the job market and the employment landscape is essential for a successful job search.

1. **Key Industries**

- **Mining and Resources**: Australia is rich in mineral resources, making mining a significant industry.
- **Healthcare**: Healthcare and medical services are in high demand, with a growing aging population.
- **Information Technology (IT)**: IT professionals, including software developers and cybersecurity experts, are in demand.
- **Education**: Australia's education sector offers employment opportunities for educators, administrators, and support staff.
- **Finance and Banking**: The financial sector includes opportunities in banking, finance, and insurance.

2. **Employment Trends**

- **Remote Work**: The COVID-19 pandemic has accelerated the adoption of remote work in Australia, opening up job opportunities across the country.

- **Gig Economy**: The gig economy is on the rise, with many Australians engaging in freelance and contract work.
- **Startups**: Australia has a thriving startup ecosystem, offering opportunities in innovation and entrepreneurship.

3. Skills in Demand

- **STEM (Science, Technology, Engineering, and Mathematics)**: STEM professionals are highly sought after in Australia.
- **Healthcare and Aged Care**: The healthcare sector has a constant demand for medical professionals and caregivers.
- **Trades and Construction**: Skilled tradespeople, such as electricians and plumbers, are in demand due to infrastructure projects.
- **Hospitality and Tourism**: With a strong tourism industry, there are opportunities in hospitality, tourism, and customer service.

4. Qualifications and Accreditation

- **Recognition of Qualifications**: Ensure that your qualifications are recognized in Australia. Some professions may require accreditation from Australian regulatory bodies.
- **Professional Associations**: Joining industry-specific professional associations can help with networking and staying updated on industry trends.

Job Search Strategies

Navigating the Australian job market requires a strategic approach. Consider these strategies for a successful job search:

1. Research and Networking

- **Market Research**: Understand the job market in your field by researching industry trends, job openings, and salary expectations.
- **Network**: Leverage your professional and personal networks to seek job referrals and introductions.
- **LinkedIn**: Create a strong LinkedIn profile to connect with professionals in your industry and join relevant groups and discussions.

2. Job Search Engines

- **Online Job Boards**: Utilize popular job search websites like Seek, Indeed, and LinkedIn Jobs to browse and apply for vacancies.
- **Company Websites**: Visit the career pages of companies you are interested in to check for job openings.

3. Recruitment Agencies

- **Register with Agencies**: Consider registering with recruitment agencies specializing in your field. They can match you with suitable job opportunities.
- **Temporary and Contract Work**: Agencies often have opportunities for temporary or contract work, which can be a foot in the door to permanent employment.

4. Job Fairs and Expos

- **Attend Events**: Job fairs and industry expos provide opportunities to meet employers, submit resumes, and learn about job openings.
- **Prepare Elevator Pitch**: Prepare a concise elevator pitch to

introduce yourself to potential employers.

5. Cold Applications

- **Direct Applications**: Don't hesitate to send direct applications to companies, even if they are not advertising vacancies. Some positions may not be publicly listed.
- **Tailor Your Resume**: Customize your resume and cover letter for each application, highlighting relevant skills and experience.

Preparing Your Job Application

Your job application, including your resume and cover letter, plays a crucial role in securing interviews and job offers. Follow these guidelines to prepare an effective application:

1. Resume (CV)

- **Contact Information**: Include your name, phone number, email address, and LinkedIn profile URL.
- **Professional Summary**: Write a concise summary that highlights your skills, experience, and career goals.
- **Work Experience**: List your work history in reverse chronological order, emphasizing accomplishments and responsibilities.
- **Education**: Detail your educational background, including degrees, institutions, and graduation dates.
- **Skills**: Highlight key skills relevant to the job, such as technical skills, language proficiency, and certifications.
- **Achievements**: Showcase notable achievements, awards, or recognition.
- **References**: Include references or state that they are available upon request.

2. Cover Letter

- **Customize Each Letter**: Tailor your cover letter for each job application, addressing the specific requirements of the role.
- **Introduction**: Begin with a strong opening that grabs the reader's attention and states the position you are applying for.
- **Body**: In the main body of the letter, demonstrate how your skills and experience align with the job requirements.
- **Highlight Achievements**: Use examples to illustrate your achievements and contributions in previous roles.
- **Closing**: Conclude with a confident closing statement, expressing your interest in an interview.

3. References

- **Select References Wisely**: Choose references who can speak to your professional abilities and character. Former employers, supervisors, or colleagues are suitable choices.
- **Request Permission**: Seek permission from your references before including their contact information in your job application.
- **Provide Details**: Include the reference's name, title, organization, email address, and phone number.

The Australian Workplace Culture

Understanding the Australian workplace culture is vital for a successful job search and career in the country:

1. Professionalism

- **Punctuality**: Arrive on time for work and appointments.
- **Communication**: Practice clear and respectful communication with colleagues and superiors.

- **Teamwork**: Collaborate effectively with team members and contribute to a positive work environment.

2. Work-Life Balance

- **Value on Balance**: Australians prioritize work-life balance and value time spent with family and pursuing hobbies.
- **Annual Leave**: Understand your entitlement to paid annual leave and other benefits.

3. Diversity and Inclusion

- **Multicultural Society**: Australia is a diverse nation, and workplaces often reflect this diversity.
- **Equal Opportunity**: Australian workplaces promote equal opportunity and inclusion.

4. Casual Dress Code

- **Smart Casual**: Many Australian workplaces have a smart-casual dress code, but it varies by industry.

5. Networking and Socializing

- **Social Events**: Participate in workplace social events and networking opportunities to build professional relationships.
- **Lunches and Coffee**: It is common to have team lunches or coffee breaks for informal discussions.

Workplace Rights and Employment Conditions

Familiarize yourself with your workplace rights and employment conditions in Australia:

1. **Fair Work Act**

- **National Employment Standards**: The Fair Work Act outlines minimum employment standards, including leave entitlements and working hours.

2. Employment Contracts

- **Written Contracts**: Employment contracts should be in writing and outline terms, conditions, and salary details.

3. Minimum Wage

- **Award Wages**: Most employees in Australia are covered by industry awards that set minimum wage rates.

4. Working Hours and Leave

- **Full-Time and Part-Time**: Understand the difference between full-time and part-time employment.
- **Leave Entitlements**: Familiarize yourself with paid leave entitlements, including annual leave, sick leave, and public holidays.

5. Superannuation

- **Mandatory Contributions**: Employers are required to make contributions to employees' superannuation funds, which provide for retirement.

Summary

The Australian job market offers a wealth of opportunities across diverse industries, but a successful job search requires careful planning and execution. By conducting thorough research, networking, preparing strong job applications, and understanding the Australian workplace culture, you can position yourself for a rewarding career in Australia.

In the chapters that follow, we will continue to explore essential aspects of your move to Australia, including cultural integration, housing, and practical tips for settling into your new life.

Settling In: Essentials for Newcomers

Settling into a new country can be both exciting and challenging. As a newcomer to Australia, there are essential aspects of life that you need to address to ensure a smooth transition and build a comfortable and fulfilling life in your new home. This chapter covers a range of essentials, from finding accommodation to adapting to the local culture and navigating day-to-day life in Australia.

Accommodation

Finding suitable accommodation is one of the first tasks you'll face as a newcomer to Australia. The type of housing you choose will depend on your preferences, budget, and family size. Here are some key points to consider:

- **Rental Market**: Australia has a competitive rental market, particularly in major cities like Sydney, Melbourne, and Brisbane. Be prepared to search diligently and consider various options.
- **Types of Housing**: You can find a variety of housing options, including apartments, houses, townhouses, and shared accommodation.
- **Location**: Consider factors like proximity to work or school, public transportation, and amenities when choosing a location.
- **Lease Terms**: Rental leases can vary in duration, but a typical lease is for 6 to 12 months. Be sure to read and understand the lease agreement before signing.
- **Rental Costs**: Rental prices can vary significantly depending on location. Ensure that your budget allows for rent and associated costs like utilities and maintenance.
- **Finding Accommodation**: Look for rental listings on real

estate websites, social media groups, and through real estate agents.

Banking and Finances

Setting up your finances in Australia is an important step in your resettlement process. Here's what you need to know:

- **Bank Accounts**: Open a bank account in Australia to manage your finances. Most banks offer various types of accounts, including savings and transaction accounts.
- **Tax File Number (TFN)**: Obtain a TFN, which is essential for tax purposes and various financial transactions.
- **Superannuation**: If you're working in Australia, your employer will contribute to your superannuation fund, which is a retirement savings account. Ensure you understand your superannuation options.
- **Currency Exchange**: Familiarize yourself with the currency exchange rates and options for transferring money to and from your home country.

Healthcare

Accessing healthcare is crucial for your well-being in Australia. Here's what you need to know:

- **Medicare**: Enroll in Medicare if you're eligible. It provides access to essential medical services and can help reduce healthcare costs.
- **Health Insurance**: Consider private health insurance to supplement Medicare coverage. It can provide additional benefits and options for treatment.
- **General Practitioner (GP)**: Find a local GP who can serve as your primary healthcare provider for routine check-ups and

non-emergency medical needs.

- **Pharmacies**: Locate nearby pharmacies where you can fill prescriptions and purchase over-the-counter medications.

Education and Childcare

If you have school-age children or need childcare services, consider the following:

- **Enrolling Your Child in School**: Ensure that your child is enrolled in a suitable school. Familiarize yourself with school holidays and term dates.
- **Childcare Services**: Research and choose appropriate childcare services if you have young children. Options include long day care, family day care, preschool, and before and after school care.
- **Education Support**: If your child requires special education support, communicate with the school and relevant professionals to ensure their needs are met.

Transportation

Getting around in Australia may require understanding the transportation options available in your area:

- **Public Transportation**: Australia has an extensive public transportation system, including buses, trains, trams, and ferries in major cities. Consider purchasing a public transportation card or pass for convenience.
- **Driving in Australia**: If you plan to drive, familiarize yourself with Australian road rules and obtain an Australian driver's license if necessary. Note that driving in Australia is on the left-hand side of the road.
- **Cycling**: Many cities have cycling paths and bike-sharing

programs, making cycling a popular and eco-friendly mode of transportation.

Cultural Integration

Adapting to the local culture and customs is essential for feeling at home in Australia:

- **Learn About Australian Culture**: Immerse yourself in Australian culture by exploring local customs, traditions, and holidays.
- **Language**: If English is not your native language, consider enrolling in English language classes to improve your communication skills.
- **Community Engagement**: Join local community groups, clubs, or associations related to your interests or cultural background to connect with others.
- **Respect Diversity**: Australia is a diverse and multicultural country. Embrace and respect the diversity of cultures and backgrounds you encounter.

Employment and Career Development

If you are seeking employment or career advancement in Australia, consider these strategies:

- **Job Search**: Continue your job search efforts, networking, and skill development to secure suitable employment.
- **Professional Development**: Stay updated with industry trends and consider professional development opportunities, workshops, and courses.
- **Networking**: Attend industry events, seminars, and workshops to expand your professional network.
- **Recognition of Qualifications**: If you have international

qualifications, explore the process of having them recognized in Australia.

Government Services and Support

Australia offers various government services and support programs to help newcomers:

- **Newcomer Support Organizations**: Seek assistance from government and non-government organizations that provide support to newcomers, including settlement services, language programs, and employment assistance.
- **Centrelink**: If you require financial support, inquire about government welfare programs through Centrelink.
- **Legal Services**: Familiarize yourself with legal services and resources available in case you need legal advice or assistance.

Safety and Emergency Services

Understanding safety and emergency services is essential for your well-being:

- **Emergency Numbers**: Know the emergency numbers, including 000 for immediate assistance in case of emergencies.
- **Fire Safety**: Familiarize yourself with fire safety procedures, especially if you live in a bushfire-prone area.
- **Health and Safety Regulations**: Be aware of health and safety regulations in your workplace and community.

Conclusion

Settling into life in Australia involves addressing various essentials, from securing accommodation to understanding the healthcare system, cultural integration, and career development. By taking these steps and gradually acclimating to your new surroundings, you can build a fulfilling and successful life in this diverse and welcoming country.

In the chapters that follow, we will continue to explore additional aspects of life in Australia, including travel and leisure, regional considerations, and practical tips for a comfortable and enjoyable stay.

Legal and Tax Considerations

Navigating the legal and tax landscape is crucial for newcomers to Australia. Understanding your rights, responsibilities, and obligations in the legal system, as well as managing your tax affairs, is essential for a smooth transition and a successful life in your new home.

Legal System in Australia

Australia operates under a legal system based on English common law principles. It has a well-developed and robust legal framework that protects individual rights and regulates various aspects of life. Here are some key legal considerations for newcomers:

1. **Visa and Immigration Laws**

- **Visa Compliance**: Ensure that you comply with the conditions of your visa. Different visas have various requirements and restrictions.
- **Visa Extensions**: Familiarize yourself with the process for extending or renewing your visa if you plan to stay longer in Australia.

2. **Legal Rights and Obligations**

- **Rule of Law**: Australia upholds the rule of law, ensuring that everyone is subject to the same legal principles and protections.
- **Individual Rights**: Understand your individual rights and freedoms, including the right to a fair trial and protection from discrimination.

3. **Legal Services**

- **Legal Assistance**: Seek legal assistance if you encounter legal issues or require advice. Legal Aid is available to eligible individuals.

- **Legal Professionals**: Australian lawyers and solicitors can provide legal representation and advice in various areas of law.

4. Property and Tenancy Laws

- **Renting Property**: Familiarize yourself with the rights and responsibilities of tenants and landlords when renting property.
- **Property Ownership**: If you plan to buy property, understand the legal process, including contracts, inspections, and settlement.

5. Family Law

- **Marriage and Divorce**: Australia has laws governing marriage, divorce, and property settlements in the event of a divorce.
- **Child Custody**: Family law also covers child custody and support arrangements.

6. Consumer Rights

- **Consumer Protections**: Consumer laws protect the rights of buyers, including warranties, refunds, and product safety.
- **Fair Trading**: The Australian Competition and Consumer Commission (ACCC) enforces fair trading and competition laws.

Legal Assistance and Resources

If you require legal assistance or information, consider the following resources:

- **Legal Aid**: Legal Aid offices in each state and territory provide free or subsidized legal advice and representation to eligible individuals.
- **Community Legal Centers**: These centers offer legal advice and support on various legal matters, including family law, employment issues, and housing disputes.
- **Australian Government Solicitor**: The Australian Government Solicitor provides legal services to government agencies and can provide advice on matters involving the federal government.
- **State and Territory Law Societies**: Contact your state or territory's Law Society for referrals to qualified lawyers and solicitors.

Taxation in Australia

Understanding the Australian tax system is essential for managing your finances and fulfilling your tax obligations. The Australian Taxation Office (ATO) oversees taxation matters, and here are key tax considerations for newcomers:

1. **Tax File Number (TFN)**

- **Apply for a TFN**: Obtain a TFN to work legally in Australia and facilitate tax-related transactions.
- **Tax File Number Declaration**: Complete a Tax File Number Declaration form when you start a new job.

2. **Types of Taxes**

- **Income Tax**: Australia has a progressive income tax system, with tax rates varying depending on your income level.

- **Goods and Services Tax (GST)**: Most goods and services in Australia are subject to a 10% GST, which is included in the sale price.
- **Capital Gains Tax (CGT)**: CGT may apply when you sell an asset, such as property or investments.

3. Employment and Taxes

- **Pay As You Go (PAYG)**: Under the PAYG system, taxes are withheld from your salary by your employer and remitted to the ATO.
- **Superannuation**: Your employer is required to make contributions to your superannuation fund, which is a retirement savings account.
- **Fringe Benefits Tax (FBT)**: If you receive non-cash benefits from your employer, such as a car or housing, FBT may apply.

4. Tax Deductions and Credits

- **Claiming Deductions**: You can claim tax deductions for work-related expenses, such as uniforms, tools, and education expenses.
- **Tax Offsets and Credits**: Explore tax offsets and credits for specific circumstances, such as the Low and Middle Income Tax Offset (LMITO).

5. Financial Year and Tax Returns

- **Tax Year**: The Australian financial year runs from July 1st to June 30th. You must file an annual tax return by October 31st if you meet certain income thresholds.

- **Online Lodgement**: Most individuals can lodge their tax returns online using the myTax platform provided by the ATO.

6. Taxation Assistance

- **Tax Agents**: You can engage a registered tax agent or accountant to help you with your tax returns and financial planning.
- **Tax Help Program**: The Tax Help program provides free assistance to eligible individuals with simple tax returns.

7. Taxation for Temporary Residents

- **Working Holiday Makers**: If you are on a working holiday visa, you may be eligible for different tax rates and benefits.
- **Temporary Residents**: Temporary residents are subject to certain tax rules, including the Departing Australia Superannuation Payment (DASP).

Summary

Understanding the legal system and tax considerations in Australia is vital for newcomers to navigate legal matters and fulfill their tax obligations. By adhering to visa requirements, seeking legal assistance when needed, and managing your finances effectively, you can ensure a smooth transition and compliance with Australian laws and regulations.

In the chapters that follow, we will continue to explore additional aspects of life in Australia, including travel and leisure, regional considerations, and practical tips for a comfortable and enjoyable stay.

Exploring Australia

Australia is a vast and diverse country, offering a wealth of natural beauty, unique wildlife, cultural experiences, and adventure opportunities. Exploring Australia is a thrilling journey, whether you're interested in the stunning landscapes, vibrant cities, or rich Indigenous heritage. In this chapter, we'll guide you through some of the must-visit destinations and activities to make the most of your time in this incredible country.

Natural Wonders

Australia is renowned for its breathtaking natural wonders, from the expansive deserts to lush rainforests. Here are some iconic destinations to explore:

1. **Uluru-Kata Tjuta National Park, Northern Territory**

- **Uluru (Ayers Rock)**: Witness the mesmerizing sunrise and sunset over Uluru, a sacred sandstone formation.
- **Kata Tjuta (The Olgas)**: Explore the domed rock formations of Kata Tjuta, known for their spiritual significance.

2. **Great Barrier Reef, Queensland**

- **Snorkeling and Diving**: Dive into the crystal-clear waters to witness the vibrant marine life of the world's largest coral reef system.
- **Whitsunday Islands**: Visit the Whitsundays for stunning beaches and opportunities to sail among the islands.

3. **The Daintree Rainforest, Queensland**

- **Ancient Rainforest**: Explore one of the world's oldest rainforests, home to diverse wildlife, lush foliage, and scenic hiking trails.

- **Cape Tribulation**: Discover the meeting point of the rainforest and the Great Barrier Reef at Cape Tribulation.

4. Blue Mountains, New South Wales

- **Scenic Landscapes**: Admire the dramatic cliffs, waterfalls, and eucalyptus forests of the Blue Mountains.
- **Hiking Trails**: Embark on hikes and bushwalks, including the popular Three Sisters and Wentworth Falls trails.

5. Kangaroo Island, South Australia

- **Wildlife Encounters**: Encounter native Australian wildlife, including kangaroos, koalas, and sea lions.
- **Remarkable Rocks**: Visit the unique rock formations known as Remarkable Rocks for stunning coastal views.

Vibrant Cities

Australia's cities offer a dynamic blend of culture, dining, entertainment, and urban experiences. Here are some cities to explore:

1. Sydney, New South Wales

- **Sydney Opera House**: Marvel at the iconic Sydney Opera House and take a guided tour of this architectural masterpiece.
- **Bondi Beach**: Relax on the sandy shores of Bondi Beach and enjoy its lively atmosphere.
- **Harbor Bridge Climb**: Embark on a thrilling climb to the top of the Sydney Harbour Bridge for panoramic views.

2. Melbourne, Victoria

- **Street Art**: Stroll through the laneways of Melbourne to discover vibrant street art and eclectic cafes.
- **Cultural Attractions**: Visit cultural hubs like the National Gallery of Victoria and the Melbourne Museum.
- **Yarra Valley**: Take a day trip to the Yarra Valley wine region for wine tasting and scenic landscapes.

3. Brisbane, Queensland

- **South Bank Parklands**: Enjoy the South Bank Parklands, with its artificial beach, gardens, and riverside dining.
- **Lone Pine Koala Sanctuary**: Get up close to koalas and other Australian wildlife at this sanctuary.
- **Moreton Island**: Explore the sandy beaches and clear waters of Moreton Island, just off the coast of Brisbane.

4. Perth, Western Australia

- **Kings Park**: Visit Kings Park and Botanic Garden for sweeping views of the city skyline and the Swan River.
- **Fremantle**: Discover the historic port city of Fremantle, known for its maritime heritage and vibrant markets.
- **Rottnest Island**: Take a ferry to Rottnest Island to see quokkas and enjoy pristine beaches.

5. Adelaide, South Australia

- **Barossa Valley**: Explore the world-famous Barossa Valley wine region for wine tasting and gourmet dining.
- **Adelaide Oval**: Catch a cricket or football match at the iconic Adelaide Oval stadium.
- **Adelaide Hills**: Drive to the Adelaide Hills for picturesque

landscapes and charming towns.

Indigenous Culture

Australia's Indigenous culture is rich and diverse, with a history spanning thousands of years. To learn about and appreciate this heritage, consider these experiences:

1. **Uluru Cultural Center, Northern Territory**

- **Indigenous Art**: Explore the cultural center to view Indigenous art and learn about the Anangu people's connection to Uluru.
- **Guided Tours**: Join guided tours led by Indigenous guides who share stories and traditions.

2. **Kakadu National Park, Northern Territory**

- **Rock Art**: Discover ancient rock art galleries in Kakadu, showcasing Indigenous art and stories.
- **Cultural Tours**: Participate in cultural tours to gain insights into the traditional practices of the Bininj/Mungguy people.

3. **Tjapukai Aboriginal Cultural Park, Queensland**

- **Interactive Experiences**: Engage in interactive experiences, including dance performances, art workshops, and boomerang throwing.
- **Dreamtime Stories**: Listen to Dreamtime stories that convey the spiritual connection of the Tjapukai people to the land.

4. **Yulara, Northern Territory**

- **Sounds of Silence Dinner**: Enjoy a unique dining experience under the outback sky, featuring Indigenous storytelling and stargazing.

- **Indigenous Astronomy**: Learn about Indigenous astronomy and celestial navigation.

Outdoor Adventures

Australia offers countless outdoor adventures for thrill-seekers and nature enthusiasts:

1. Great Ocean Road, Victoria

- **Twelve Apostles**: Witness the dramatic rock formations known as the Twelve Apostles along this iconic coastal drive.
- **Surfing**: Try your hand at surfing on the renowned Bells Beach.

2. Cradle Mountain-Lake St Clair National Park, Tasmania

- **Hiking**: Embark on the Overland Track, a multi-day hiking trail through stunning alpine landscapes.
- **Wildlife**: Encounter unique Tasmanian wildlife, including wombats and wallabies.

3. Cairns, Queensland

- **White-Water Rafting**: Experience the thrill of white-water rafting on the Tully River.
- **Skydiving**: Take a leap and go skydiving over the Great Barrier Reef for breathtaking views.

4. The Kimberley, Western Australia

- **Scenic Flights**: Take a scenic flight over the rugged landscapes of The Kimberley, known for its dramatic gorges and waterfalls.

- **Four-Wheel Driving**: Explore remote areas by four-wheel driving along the Gibb River Road.

5. Tongariro Alpine Crossing, New Zealand (Side Trip)

- **Hike the Tongariro**: Take a side trip to New Zealand's North Island and hike the Tongariro Alpine Crossing, one of the world's best day hikes.
- **Geothermal Wonders**: Explore the geothermal wonders of Rotorua and relax in hot springs.

Culinary Experiences

Australian cuisine reflects its multicultural society and diverse landscapes. Sample local flavors and culinary traditions:

1. Seafood in Sydney

- **Sydney Fish Market**: Visit the Sydney Fish Market for an array of fresh seafood options.
- **Pubs and Restaurants**: Dine at waterfront restaurants and traditional pubs for seafood specialties.

2. Barbecue (Barbie) Culture

- **Outdoor Barbecues**: Experience the quintessential Australian barbecue culture by grilling meats and vegetables in scenic parks.
- **Sausage Sizzles**: Attend charity sausage sizzles often held at hardware stores and community events.

3. Wine Tasting in South Australia

- **Wine Regions**: Explore South Australia's wine regions, including the Barossa Valley and McLaren Vale, for wine tastings and vineyard tours.

- **Local Produce**: Pair your wine with local produce and gourmet dishes at winery restaurants.

4. Melbourne's Café Culture

- **Coffee and Brunch**: Melbourne is known for its café culture, so indulge in quality coffee and brunch at laneway cafes.
- **International Flavors**: Enjoy international cuisine and multicultural food markets throughout the city.

5. Bush Tucker

- **Indigenous Cuisine**: Taste Indigenous ingredients and traditional dishes, known as bush tucker, in specialized restaurants and tours.
- **Bushtucker Tours**: Join bushtucker tours to learn about the native plants and animals used in Indigenous cooking.

Travel Tips

To make the most of your exploration of Australia, keep these travel tips in mind:

- **Travel Insurance**: Consider purchasing travel insurance to cover unexpected events, such as medical emergencies and trip cancellations.
- **Transportation**: Research transportation options, including domestic flights, trains, buses, and car rentals, depending on your travel itinerary.
- **Weather**: Be mindful of Australia's diverse climate and pack accordingly for each region and season.
- **Responsible Tourism**: Practice responsible tourism by

respecting local environments and wildlife, and adhering to conservation guidelines.

- **Local Etiquette**: Familiarize yourself with local customs and etiquette, including tipping practices and cultural sensitivities.
- **Emergency Contact**: Save emergency contact numbers, including medical facilities and consular services, in case of emergencies.

Conclusion

Exploring Australia is an incredible adventure, offering a vast array of natural wonders, vibrant cities, Indigenous culture, outdoor activities, and culinary experiences. Whether you're drawn to the unique wildlife of the outback, the bustling streets of urban hubs, or the serene beauty of coastal landscapes, Australia has something to offer every traveler. Embrace the diversity and richness of this beautiful country as you embark on your journey of discovery.

In the chapters that follow, we will continue to explore additional aspects of life in Australia, including regional considerations, practical tips for a comfortable stay, and important resources for newcomers.

Staying Connected

Maintaining connections and building a support network is essential for newcomers to Australia. Staying connected with family, friends, and the local community can enhance your well-being, ease your transition, and enrich your experience in this new country. In this chapter, we will explore various ways to foster connections and stay engaged with the people around you.

Family and Friends

Moving to a new country often means leaving behind loved ones in your home country. Here are ways to stay connected with family and friends, even when you're far from home:

1. **Video Calls**

- **Online Platforms**: Utilize video calling platforms like Zoom, Skype, or FaceTime to have face-to-face conversations with loved ones.
- **Regular Schedule**: Establish a regular schedule for video calls to maintain a sense of closeness.

2. **Social Media**

- **Facebook**: Stay connected through Facebook to share updates, photos, and messages with friends and family.
- **Instagram**: Share snapshots of your life in Australia on Instagram and follow your loved ones' posts as well.

3. **Messaging Apps**

- **WhatsApp**: Use WhatsApp for instant messaging, voice calls, and sharing multimedia with contacts worldwide.
- **Messenger**: Connect through Facebook Messenger for both

text and video chats.

4. Email

- **Regular Updates**: Send regular email updates to provide details about your new life and experiences.
- **Newsletters**: Consider creating email newsletters to share highlights and photos.

5. Virtual Events

- **Celebrations**: Participate in virtual celebrations for birthdays, holidays, and special occasions.
- **Online Games**: Play online games or participate in virtual activities together.

Building a Local Support Network

Creating connections within your local community can help you adapt to your new surroundings and provide a sense of belonging. Here's how to build a local support network:

1. Attend Community Events

- **Festivals**: Attend local festivals, cultural events, and community fairs to meet residents and engage in cultural celebrations.
- **Meetups**: Join online platforms like Meetup.com to find groups and events that align with your interests.

2. Volunteer

- **Volunteer Organizations**: Contribute your time and skills to local volunteer organizations, which can lead to meaningful connections.

- **Causes You Care About**: Choose causes you are passionate about to connect with like-minded individuals.

3. Local Clubs and Associations

- **Sports Clubs**: Join local sports clubs or teams to participate in activities you enjoy.
- **Hobby Groups**: Seek out hobbyist groups, such as photography, gardening, or book clubs, that align with your interests.

4. Language and Cultural Classes

- **Language Classes**: Enroll in language classes to improve your communication skills and connect with classmates.
- **Cultural Centers**: Visit cultural centers and institutions to learn about the heritage of your new community.

5. Neighborhood Activities

- **Neighborhood Watch**: Join or start a neighborhood watch group to foster connections with neighbors and enhance safety.
- **Block Parties**: Organize or attend block parties and neighborhood gatherings to get to know your community.

Social and Support Groups

Staying connected through social and support groups can provide a sense of belonging and assist with various aspects of your life in Australia:

1. Expat Groups

- **Online Communities**: Join expat communities and forums

to connect with others who have relocated to Australia.

- **Local Expat Clubs**: Seek out local expat clubs and associations that organize social events and provide support.

2. Parenting Groups

- **Playgroups**: If you have children, join playgroups to meet other parents and arrange playdates.
- **Parenting Classes**: Attend parenting classes and workshops to connect with fellow parents.

3. Professional Networks

- **Industry Associations**: Join industry-specific associations and networking events related to your profession.
- **LinkedIn**: Connect with professionals in your field on LinkedIn to expand your network.

4. Mental Health and Well-being Groups

- **Support Groups**: Consider joining support groups or therapy sessions to address mental health concerns or the challenges of relocation.
- **Exercise Classes**: Participate in exercise classes, yoga, or meditation groups to promote mental and emotional well-being.

Religious and Faith Communities

If you have religious or spiritual beliefs, connecting with a local faith community can provide a strong support network:

1. Places of Worship

- **Attend Services**: Visit local churches, temples, mosques, synagogues, or other places of worship to connect with fellow believers.

- **Participate in Activities**: Engage in religious or spiritual activities, such as prayer groups, meditation sessions, or study circles.

2. Religious Organizations

- **Community Outreach**: Get involved in community outreach programs or charity work organized by religious organizations.
- **Festivals and Celebrations**: Attend religious festivals and celebrations to experience cultural and spiritual traditions.

Language Exchange

Language exchange programs provide an opportunity to improve your language skills while connecting with people from different backgrounds:

1. Language Exchange Partners

- **Tandem Learning**: Find language exchange partners who want to learn your native language in exchange for teaching you their language.
- **Language Exchange Apps**: Use language exchange apps and websites to connect with language learners in your area.

2. Language Classes

- **Community Classes**: Enroll in community language classes or conversation groups to practice and make new friends.
- **University Programs**: Some universities and cultural centers offer language courses and conversation partners.

Online Communities

The internet offers countless online communities and social platforms to connect with people who share your interests or background:

1. **Social Media Groups**

- **Facebook Groups**: Join local or interest-based Facebook groups to connect with people in your area.
- **Reddit**: Explore Reddit communities related to your hobbies, interests, or location.

2. **Online Forums**

- **Niche Forums**: Participate in online forums and discussion boards related to your interests, profession, or hobbies.
- **Expatriate Forums**: Engage in expatriate forums to connect with others who have relocated to Australia.

Cultural and International Centers

Many cities in Australia have cultural and international centers that offer resources and events for newcomers:

1. **Multicultural Centers**

- **Language Classes**: Enroll in language classes offered by multicultural centers to improve your language skills.
- **Cultural Events**: Attend cultural events and festivals to learn about various cultures and traditions.

2. **Embassies and Consulates**

- **Diplomatic Events**: Attend events organized by your country's embassy or consulate to connect with fellow nationals.
- **Consular Services**: Utilize consular services and support in

case of emergencies or documentation needs.

Maintaining Long-Distance Relationships

If you have friends and family in different time zones, maintaining long-distance relationships can be challenging. Here are some strategies:

1. **Scheduling**

- **Coordinate Time Zones**: Find suitable times for calls and conversations by considering time zone differences.
- **Regular Check-Ins**: Schedule regular check-in times to maintain a consistent connection.

2. **Shared Experiences**

- **Virtual Experiences**: Share virtual experiences, such as watching the same movie or reading the same book, and discuss them later.
- **Online Games**: Play online multiplayer games together to bond over a shared activity.

3. **Planning Visits**

- **Visit Each Other**: Plan visits to each other's countries to spend quality time together in person.
- **Vacation Together**: Arrange vacations to meet at a neutral destination for a shared adventure.

4. **Communication Apps**

- **Messaging Apps**: Use messaging apps to send quick updates and stay in touch throughout the day.
- **Email Updates**: Send periodic email updates with photos

and stories of your life in Australia.

Overcoming Language Barriers

If you are adjusting to a new language, here are strategies to overcome language barriers and connect with others:

1. **Language Classes**

- **Enroll in Language Classes**: Take formal language classes to improve your proficiency.
- **Language Apps**: Use language-learning apps to practice speaking, listening, and reading.

2. **Practice Conversations**

- **Language Exchange**: Engage in language exchange partnerships to practice conversational skills.
- **Join Conversation Groups**: Attend language conversation groups or meetups to interact with native speakers.

3. **Cultural Immersion**

- **Immerse Yourself**: Surround yourself with the local language through media, books, and cultural events.
- **Local Communities**: Join local communities and events that use the language you're learning.

Conclusion

Staying connected in a new country is crucial for emotional well-being, support, and a sense of belonging. Whether you're reaching out to family and friends back home, building a local support network, or connecting with like-minded individuals, there are numerous avenues to foster meaningful relationships. Embrace the opportunities to engage with others, share experiences, and create a fulfilling life in Australia.

In the chapters that follow, we will continue to explore additional aspects of life in Australia, including regional considerations, practical tips for a comfortable stay, and important resources for newcomers.

Overcoming Challenges

Moving to a new country, like Australia, is a thrilling adventure filled with opportunities for growth and self-discovery. However, it also comes with its fair share of challenges. From adjusting to a new culture and navigating bureaucratic processes to managing homesickness and coping with unexpected setbacks, newcomers may face various obstacles. In this chapter, we will explore common challenges faced by those moving to Australia and provide strategies for overcoming them.

1. Cultural Adjustment

Challenge: Adjusting to a new culture can be overwhelming. Differences in language, customs, social norms, and daily routines may lead to culture shock and feelings of isolation.

Strategies:

- **Cultural Sensitivity**: Educate yourself about Australian culture, customs, and etiquette. Respect for local customs can help you integrate more smoothly.
- **Language Skills**: If English is not your native language, invest time in improving your language skills through classes, language apps, and immersion.
- **Cultural Exchange**: Engage in cultural exchange activities and seek opportunities to learn from local residents about their customs and traditions.
- **Support Networks**: Connect with other newcomers and expats who are experiencing similar cultural adjustments. They can offer insights and support.

2. Homesickness

Challenge: Missing your home country, family, and friends is a common challenge when moving abroad. Homesickness can lead to feelings of sadness and loneliness.

Strategies:

- **Stay Connected**: Maintain regular contact with loved ones through video calls, messaging apps, and social media to bridge the distance.
- **Create a Familiar Environment**: Decorate your home with items that remind you of your home country to create a sense of comfort.
- **Establish Routines**: Establish daily routines and traditions that provide a sense of continuity and stability in your new environment.
- **Meet Fellow Expats**: Connect with other expats who understand the challenges of homesickness and can offer support.

3. Employment Challenges

Challenge: Finding a job in a new country, especially one with different job markets and requirements, can be daunting. Navigating job searches, interviews, and professional networks can be challenging.

Strategies:

- **Job Research**: Thoroughly research the job market in your field and location. Understand the qualifications and certifications required.
- **Networking**: Attend networking events, join industry associations, and use professional networking platforms like LinkedIn to build connections.
- **Tailored Resumes**: Customize your resume and cover letter for each job application to highlight your relevant skills and

experiences.

- **Seek Guidance**: Consider career counseling or job placement services offered by immigrant support organizations or government agencies.

4. Housing and Accommodation

Challenge: Finding suitable housing in a new country can be complex, particularly in competitive rental markets. Understanding rental agreements and tenancy laws may also pose challenges.

Strategies:

- **Research Areas**: Research neighborhoods and suburbs to identify areas that align with your preferences and budget.
- **Rental Assistance**: Seek advice from real estate agents, relocation services, or community organizations that specialize in assisting newcomers with housing.
- **Understanding Tenancy Laws**: Familiarize yourself with Australian tenancy laws to know your rights and responsibilities as a tenant.
- **Temporary Housing**: Consider temporary housing options, such as serviced apartments or short-term rentals, while you search for a permanent home.

5. Healthcare Access

Challenge: Accessing healthcare in a new country may involve understanding a different healthcare system, securing health insurance, and finding suitable healthcare providers.

Strategies:

- **Health Insurance**: Research and purchase appropriate health insurance coverage to ensure you have access to necessary healthcare services.

- **Medical Facilities**: Locate nearby medical facilities, general practitioners (GPs), and specialists. Ask for recommendations from locals or expats.
- **Understand the System**: Familiarize yourself with the Australian healthcare system, including how to make appointments and obtain prescriptions.
- **Emergency Contacts**: Keep a list of emergency contacts, including local hospitals, clinics, and healthcare hotlines.

6. Financial Management

Challenge: Managing finances in a new country involves understanding currency, banking systems, taxes, and budgeting for the cost of living.

Strategies:

- **Banking Setup**: Open a local bank account to simplify financial transactions and minimize currency exchange fees.
- **Budgeting**: Create a budget that considers your income, expenses, and savings goals. Adjust it as needed to adapt to the cost of living in Australia.
- **Taxation**: Familiarize yourself with Australian tax laws and filing requirements. Consider consulting a tax professional for guidance.
- **Currency Exchange**: Monitor exchange rates and consider cost-effective methods for transferring funds between your home country and Australia.

7. Social Integration

Challenge: Building a social life in a new country can be challenging, especially when you're far from familiar social circles. Loneliness and social isolation can be daunting.

Strategies:

- **Participate in Activities**: Engage in activities and hobbies you enjoy, whether it's sports, arts, or volunteering, to meet people with similar interests.
- **Attend Social Events**: Attend social events, gatherings, and meetups to connect with locals and fellow expats.
- **Language Classes**: Take language classes or courses related to your interests to meet people and improve your skills.
- **Online Communities**: Join online expat or community forums and social media groups to find like-minded individuals and stay updated on local events.

8. Legal and Immigration Challenges

Challenge: Navigating the legal and immigration processes in a new country can be complex, with various visa requirements, regulations, and documentation.

Strategies:

- **Legal Advice**: Seek legal advice or consult with immigration experts to understand visa requirements and comply with immigration laws.
- **Documentation**: Keep important documents organized and up to date, including visas, passports, and any permits required for your stay.
- **Visa Renewal**: Stay informed about the expiration date of your visa and start the renewal process well in advance, if necessary.
- **Compliance**: Always adhere to the conditions of your visa, as non-compliance could result in legal issues and visa cancellations.

9. Childcare and Education

Challenge: If you have children, ensuring their well-being and education in a new country can be a priority and a challenge. Finding suitable childcare and understanding the education system may require research and adjustments.

Strategies:

- **Research Schools**: Research local schools and educational institutions, considering their curriculum, reputation, and proximity to your home.
- **Childcare Services**: Explore childcare options, such as daycare centers, after-school programs, and playgroups, if needed.
- **Parent Support Groups**: Connect with parent support groups and associations to share experiences and receive guidance on parenting in Australia.
- **School Enrollment**: Familiarize yourself with the enrollment process and school requirements, and ensure your child's documentation is in order.

10. Emergency Preparedness

Challenge: Being prepared for emergencies, such as natural disasters or health crises, is vital. Understanding emergency procedures and knowing how to access help can be challenging in a new country.

Strategies:

- **Emergency Contacts**: Keep a list of emergency contacts, including local authorities, healthcare providers, and embassy or consulate contacts.
- **Emergency Kit**: Prepare an emergency kit with essentials like water, non-perishable food, first-aid supplies, and important documents.
- **Stay Informed**: Stay updated on local news, weather alerts,

and safety procedures for various emergency scenarios.

- **Local Authorities**: Familiarize yourself with local emergency response agencies and their contact information.

Conclusion

Moving to Australia is a life-changing experience that can be both rewarding and challenging. While challenges are an inevitable part of the journey, they can be overcome with resilience, resourcefulness, and a support network. By acknowledging these challenges, seeking assistance when needed, and staying adaptable, you can thrive in your new home. Remember that you're not alone in your experiences, and there are resources and communities ready to support you as you navigate the challenges of life in Australia.

In the chapters that follow, we will continue to explore additional aspects of life in Australia, including regional considerations, practical tips for a comfortable stay, and important resources for newcomers.

Citizenship and Permanent Residency

Gaining citizenship or permanent residency in Australia is a significant milestone for many newcomers. It offers long-term stability, access to a range of benefits, and the opportunity to fully integrate into Australian society. In this chapter, we will explore the pathways to Australian citizenship and permanent residency, the benefits of each, and the application processes.

1. Understanding Permanent Residency

Permanent Residency (PR) is a status that allows you to live and work in Australia indefinitely. It is often considered a stepping stone to Australian citizenship, as it provides a stable legal status in the country. Here are some key aspects of PR:

- **Visa Categories**: PR can be obtained through various visa categories, such as skilled migration, family reunion, and humanitarian programs.
- **Benefits**: PR holders are entitled to many of the same rights and benefits as Australian citizens, including access to healthcare, education, and social services.
- **Travel Rights**: PR allows you to travel in and out of Australia without the need for additional visas. However, you must return within a specified period to maintain your PR status.
- **Eligibility for Citizenship**: PR is a common prerequisite for becoming an Australian citizen. You generally need to be a PR holder for a specified period before applying for citizenship.

2. Pathways to Permanent Residency

There are several pathways to obtaining permanent residency in Australia. The most common include:

a. **Skilled Migration**

- **Skilled Independent Visa (subclass 189)**: This visa is for skilled workers who are not sponsored by an employer, state, or family member. To qualify, you must meet specific skill and point requirements.
- **Skilled Nominated Visa (subclass 190)**: State or territory governments nominate skilled workers for this visa. You must be nominated by a state or territory and meet the skill and point requirements.
- **Skilled Regional (Provisional) Visa (subclass 491)**: This visa allows skilled workers to live and work in regional areas of Australia. It requires nomination by a state or territory government or sponsorship by an eligible family member living in a designated area.

b. **Family Reunion**

- **Partner Visa (subclass 820/801)**: This visa is for spouses or de facto partners of Australian citizens, permanent residents, or eligible New Zealand citizens.
- **Parent Visa (various subclasses)**: Parents of Australian citizens, permanent residents, or eligible New Zealand citizens can apply for parent visas. These visas have long waiting periods and substantial financial requirements.

c. **Employer Nomination**

- **Employer Nomination Scheme (ENS) Visa (subclass 186)**: This visa is for skilled workers nominated by an Australian employer. It has both temporary and permanent residency pathways.

- **Regional Employer Sponsored Visa (subclass 494)**: Skilled workers can be sponsored by an employer in regional Australia for this visa. It can lead to permanent residency.

d. Humanitarian Programs

- **Refugee and Humanitarian Visas**: Individuals granted refugee or humanitarian visas may eventually become eligible for permanent residency.

e. Business and Investment Visas

- **Business Innovation and Investment Visa (subclass 888)**: This visa is for individuals who have established a successful business or invested a substantial amount in Australia.
- **Investor Visa (subclass 891)**: Investors who have maintained an investment in Australia for a specified period may be eligible for this visa.

f. Other Special Eligibility Categories

- **Distinguished Talent Visa (subclass 858)**: This visa is for individuals with exceptional talent or outstanding achievements in a specific field.
- **Global Talent Visa (subclass 858)**: Designed to attract high-caliber individuals in targeted industries, this visa offers a streamlined pathway to PR.

3. Benefits of Permanent Residency

Obtaining permanent residency in Australia comes with a range of benefits:

- **Stability**: PR provides long-term stability, allowing you to live and work in Australia indefinitely.

- **Social Services**: PR holders have access to Australia's comprehensive social services, including healthcare, education, and social welfare.
- **Work Rights**: PR allows you to work for any employer in Australia without the need for sponsorship.
- **Travel Flexibility**: You can travel in and out of Australia as often as you like during the validity of your PR visa.
- **Sponsor Family**: PR holders can sponsor eligible family members for permanent residency.
- **Path to Citizenship**: PR is a common pathway to Australian citizenship, which provides additional rights and privileges.

4. Australian Citizenship

Becoming an Australian citizen is the ultimate goal for many permanent residents. Citizenship offers full participation in Australian society, including the right to vote, hold public office, and obtain an Australian passport. Here are the key aspects of Australian citizenship:

- **Residency Requirement**: To apply for Australian citizenship, you generally need to have been a permanent resident for at least four years, including one year as a PR holder.
- **Good Character**: Applicants must demonstrate good character and a commitment to Australian values.
- **Citizenship Test**: Most applicants aged 18-60 are required to pass a citizenship test covering Australian history, culture, and values.
- **Citizenship Ceremony**: Once your application is approved, you will be invited to attend a citizenship ceremony where you pledge your loyalty to Australia.

5. Benefits of Australian Citizenship

Becoming an Australian citizen comes with several advantages:

- **Voting Rights**: Australian citizens have the right to vote in federal, state, and local elections, influencing the country's political landscape.
- **Eligibility for Public Office**: Citizens can run for public office and serve in various government positions.
- **Australian Passport**: Citizens are entitled to an Australian passport, which offers visa-free or visa-on-arrival access to many countries.
- **Access to Government Services**: Citizenship ensures access to government services and benefits not available to non-citizens.
- **Full Integration**: As a citizen, you are fully integrated into Australian society and have a stronger sense of belonging.

6. Applying for Permanent Residency and Citizenship

The application processes for permanent residency and citizenship can be complex and require careful documentation and adherence to specific requirements. Here is an overview of the general steps:

Applying for Permanent Residency (PR):

- **Select the Appropriate Visa**: Determine the most suitable PR visa category based on your circumstances and eligibility.
- **Gather Documentation**: Collect the required documents, which may include proof of identity, qualifications, skills assessments, and character references.
- **Lodge Your Application**: Submit your application online through the Department of Home Affairs website or through a registered migration agent.
- **Health and Character Checks**: Undergo medical

examinations and provide police clearance certificates as part
of the character assessment.

- **Visa Grant**: Once your application is approved, you will
receive a visa grant, allowing you to live and work in Australia
as a permanent resident.

Applying for Australian Citizenship:

- **Meet Residency Requirements**: Ensure you meet the
residency requirement of being a PR holder for at least four
years, including one year as a PR holder.
- **Prepare Documentation**: Gather the necessary
documentation, such as identity documents, proof of
residency, and evidence of good character.
- **Pass the Citizenship Test**: Study for and pass the citizenship
test, which assesses your knowledge of Australia's history,
culture, and values.
- **Lodge Your Application**: Submit your citizenship
application online or by mail, along with the required fees
and supporting documents.
- **Citizenship Ceremony**: Attend a citizenship ceremony if
your application is approved. This is the final step in the
citizenship process.
- **Receive Citizenship Certificate**: After taking the citizenship
pledge, you will be presented with an Australian citizenship
certificate.

7. Maintaining Permanent Residency and Citizenship

Once you obtain permanent residency or citizenship, it is essential
to understand the obligations and responsibilities associated with your
status:

Permanent Residency (PR):

- **Residency Requirement**: To maintain your PR status, you must reside in Australia for at least two years out of the last five years. Extended periods of absence may lead to visa cancellations.
- **Renewal and Citizenship**: Consider applying for Australian citizenship after meeting the eligibility criteria, as it offers additional security and privileges.

Australian Citizenship:

- **Reside in Australia**: To maintain Australian citizenship, you are not required to reside in the country continuously. However, residing in Australia demonstrates your commitment to being an active member of the community.
- **Dual Citizenship**: Australia allows dual citizenship, so you can maintain your citizenship in your home country if it permits dual nationality.
- **Contribute to Society**: As an Australian citizen, you are encouraged to actively participate in Australian society, uphold its values, and contribute to the community.

8. Dual Citizenship

Australia generally allows its citizens to hold dual citizenship, which means you can be a citizen of both Australia and another country simultaneously. However, it's essential to check the laws and regulations of your home country regarding dual citizenship, as some countries may not permit it. Before applying for Australian citizenship, consider the implications for your existing citizenship.

9. Conclusion

Obtaining permanent residency and, eventually, Australian citizenship is a significant accomplishment for newcomers to Australia. These statuses provide stability, access to benefits, and the opportunity to fully engage in Australian society. Whether you are pursuing permanent residency for long-term residency or aiming for citizenship to become an active member of the Australian community, understanding the pathways and requirements is essential. The decision to pursue permanent residency or citizenship is a significant one, and it should align with your long-term goals and aspirations in Australia.

In the chapters that follow, we will continue to explore additional aspects of life in Australia, including regional considerations, practical tips for a comfortable stay, and important resources for newcomers.

Future Planning

As you settle into your new life in Australia, it's essential to plan for the future to ensure your long-term well-being and success in this diverse and dynamic country. Future planning encompasses a wide range of aspects, including career development, financial security, family goals, and personal aspirations. In this chapter, we will delve into key areas of future planning to help you navigate your journey effectively.

1. Career and Professional Development

a. Skill Enhancement

Continuously improving your skills and qualifications is essential for career growth. Consider the following:

- **Further Education**: Explore opportunities for advanced degrees or certifications in your field.
- **Professional Training**: Attend workshops, seminars, and conferences to stay updated on industry trends.
- **Networking**: Build and maintain a professional network to access job opportunities and career advice.

b. Career Advancement

- **Set Goals**: Define clear career goals and objectives to guide your professional development.
- **Seek Mentoring**: Find a mentor or coach who can provide guidance and support as you advance in your career.
- **Performance Reviews**: Engage actively in performance evaluations with your employer to identify areas for improvement.

c. Entrepreneurship and Business Ownership

- **Business Ideas**: If you have entrepreneurial aspirations, explore opportunities for starting or investing in a business in Australia.
- **Market Research**: Conduct thorough market research to understand the local business landscape and consumer preferences.
- **Financial Planning**: Develop a robust business plan and financial strategy to ensure the sustainability of your venture.

2. Financial Security
a. Savings and Investments

- **Emergency Fund**: Build an emergency fund to cover unexpected expenses, such as medical bills or job loss.
- **Invest Wisely**: Consider various investment options, such as stocks, bonds, real estate, and retirement accounts, to grow your wealth.
- **Diversification**: Diversify your investments to reduce risk and achieve long-term financial stability.

b. Budgeting and Financial Planning

- **Create a Budget**: Develop a monthly budget that outlines your income, expenses, and savings goals.
- **Financial Planner**: Consider consulting a financial planner for personalized advice and investment strategies.
- **Debt Management**: Manage and reduce any outstanding debts, such as credit card balances or loans.

3. Family and Personal Goals
a. Family Planning

- **Children's Education**: Plan for your children's education by exploring school options and setting up education funds.
- **Homeownership**: If you aspire to own a home, research the real estate market and mortgage options.
- **Estate Planning**: Establish a will, power of attorney, and other legal documents to ensure your family's financial security.

b. Personal Aspirations

- **Travel and Exploration**: Plan and budget for travel within Australia and abroad to explore new destinations.
- **Hobbies and Interests**: Pursue hobbies and interests that bring you joy and personal fulfillment.
- **Health and Well-being**: Prioritize physical and mental health by maintaining a healthy lifestyle and seeking regular medical check-ups.

4. Education and Skill Development
a. Continued Learning

- **Lifelong Learning**: Embrace lifelong learning by taking courses or workshops that interest you.
- **Language Skills**: If English is not your first language, continue to improve your language skills for better communication and job prospects.
- **Online Learning**: Explore online learning platforms that offer a wide range of courses in various fields.

b. Children's Education

- **Educational Support**: Provide support and resources for

your children's education, including tutoring or
extracurricular activities.

- **Career Guidance**: Help your children explore potential
  career paths and educational opportunities.

5. Retirement Planning
a. Superannuation

- **Understand Superannuation**: Learn about Australia's
  retirement savings system, including employer contributions
  and investment options.
- **Contribute Adequately**: Consider making additional
  voluntary contributions to your superannuation fund to
  secure a comfortable retirement.
- **Retirement Age**: Be aware of the retirement age in Australia
  and plan your retirement accordingly.

b. Financial Preparation

- **Retirement Budget**: Create a retirement budget that
  outlines your expected expenses and income sources.
- **Seek Advice**: Consult with a financial advisor or retirement
  planner to ensure your financial security during retirement.

6. Legal and Immigration Considerations
a. Visa Renewal and Compliance

- **Visa Expiry**: Keep track of your visa expiry date and initiate
  the renewal process in a timely manner.
- **Compliance**: Ensure that you adhere to the conditions of
  your visa to maintain your legal status in Australia.
- **Permanent Residency**: If you are a permanent resident, plan

for the eventual acquisition of Australian citizenship.

b. Citizenship Planning

- **Eligibility**: Determine when you become eligible to apply for Australian citizenship based on your permanent residency status.
- **Application Process**: Familiarize yourself with the citizenship application process, including the citizenship test and interview.

7. Emergency Preparedness
a. Health and Safety

- **Health Insurance**: Maintain adequate health insurance coverage for yourself and your family.
- **Emergency Contacts**: Keep a list of emergency contacts, including local medical facilities and emergency services.

b. Natural Disasters

- **Stay Informed**: Be aware of potential natural disasters in your region and stay informed about emergency procedures.
- **Emergency Kit**: Prepare an emergency kit with essentials such as food, water, first-aid supplies, and important documents.

8. Community Engagement
a. Social Networks

- **Maintain Connections**: Stay connected with your local community, neighbors, and friends to build a support system.
- **Volunteer**: Consider volunteering or participating in

community activities to give back and connect with others.

b. **Advocacy and Involvement**

- **Advocate for Change**: Get involved in advocacy or social causes that are important to you and your community.
- **Participate in Local Events**: Attend local events, festivals, and cultural celebrations to embrace the diversity of Australian society.

9. Conclusion

Future planning is an ongoing process that evolves with your changing circumstances and goals. By taking proactive steps to plan for your career, financial security, family aspirations, personal development, and legal status, you can navigate your journey in Australia with confidence and resilience. Stay adaptable and open to new opportunities, and seek professional guidance when needed. As you continue to grow and thrive in Australia, remember that careful planning today can lead to a brighter and more secure future tomorrow.

In the chapters that follow, we will continue to explore additional aspects of life in Australia, including regional considerations, practical tips for a comfortable stay, and important resources for newcomers.

Conclusion

Congratulations on reaching the conclusion of this comprehensive guide on moving to and living in Australia. Your journey has taken you through a wealth of information, from the initial decision to move to Australia, understanding the visa process, and settling into your new life. As you reflect on the wealth of knowledge you've gained, let's take a moment to recap some key takeaways and offer final thoughts to guide you on your path forward.

Reflecting on Your Journey

Your decision to move to Australia was likely filled with a mix of excitement, anticipation, and perhaps a touch of anxiety. Whether you embarked on this journey for career opportunities, personal growth, or a change of scenery, you've demonstrated resilience and a thirst for adventure. Moving to a new country is a remarkable endeavor, and it's important to acknowledge and celebrate your courage in taking this significant step.

The Visa Journey

Understanding the Australian visa system is crucial, and you've navigated it admirably. You've learned about various visa categories, eligibility criteria, and the application process. From skilled migration to family reunion, humanitarian programs, and business visas, you've explored the diverse pathways available to newcomers. Remember that the visa journey is a vital part of your Australian adventure, and staying informed and compliant is essential to maintaining your legal status.

Settling In and Thriving

Settling into your new life in Australia involves more than just physical relocation; it's about finding your sense of belonging and building a fulfilling life. You've discovered how to secure accommodation, manage your finances, access healthcare, and educate your children. You've also explored the rich tapestry of Australian culture, regional diversity, and recreational opportunities.

Building Connections

Connecting with others is a cornerstone of your journey. You've learned how to establish social networks, make friends, and engage with your local community. You've embraced the chance to meet people from different backgrounds and cultures, enriching your own experience while contributing to the vibrant tapestry of Australian society.

Future Planning

Looking ahead, you've begun to consider your long-term goals and aspirations in Australia. Whether you're planning for career advancement, financial security, family growth, or retirement, future planning is essential. By setting clear goals, seeking ongoing education, and prioritizing your health and well-being, you're laying the foundation for a prosperous future.

Legal and Immigration Considerations

Maintaining compliance with Australian immigration laws is a top priority. You've learned about visa renewal, permanent residency, and the pathway to Australian citizenship. It's vital to stay informed about the requirements and responsibilities associated with your legal status to ensure a smooth and secure journey in Australia.

Emergency Preparedness and Community Engagement

Australia's unique geography and climate bring both beauty and challenges. You've explored the importance of emergency preparedness, from health and safety to natural disaster readiness. Being well-informed and proactive can make all the difference in times of crisis.

Additionally, you've discovered the value of community engagement and social involvement. By actively participating in local events, volunteering, and advocating for causes that matter to you, you're not only enriching your own life but contributing to the broader community.

The Continuation of Your Australian Adventure

As you move forward on your Australian adventure, keep in mind that this guide is just the beginning. Your journey will continue to evolve, presenting new opportunities and challenges along the way. Embrace the spirit of curiosity and adaptability that brought you to Australia, and remember that you're never alone. Australia's welcoming and diverse community is here to support you, and a world of experiences awaits you.

Seeking Professional Guidance

Throughout your journey, you may find it beneficial to seek professional guidance. Whether you require legal advice, financial planning, or career coaching, don't hesitate to reach out to experts who can provide valuable insights and assistance tailored to your specific needs.

Celebrating Diversity

Australia's multiculturalism is one of its greatest strengths. As you settle into your new life, take the time to celebrate the rich diversity of cultures, traditions, and perspectives that make up this vibrant nation. Engage in cultural exchange, learn from others, and contribute your own unique background to the Australian mosaic.

A World of Possibilities

In closing, remember that your journey in Australia is a testament to your resilience, adaptability, and the endless possibilities that await you in this remarkable country. Whether you're building a career, nurturing your family, or exploring new horizons, Australia offers a world of opportunities for growth and fulfillment.

We wish you the very best in your continued adventure in Australia. May your days be filled with discovery, your nights with dreams, and your heart with the warmth of this land and its people. Embrace every moment, cherish every experience, and savor the unique beauty of your Australian journey.

Appendix

In this appendix, you will find additional resources and information to support your journey as a newcomer to Australia. These resources cover a wide range of topics, from government agencies and immigrant support organizations to useful websites, apps, and publications.

1. Government Resources

- **Department of Home Affairs**: The official website for immigration and visas in Australia provides information on visa options, application processes, and immigration policies. Website: https://immi.homeaffairs.gov.au/
- **Australian Government Services**: Access a wide range of government services, including healthcare, education, and legal information. Website: https://www.australia.gov.au/
- **Department of Health**: Find information on Australia's healthcare system, including Medicare and health insurance. Website: https://www.health.gov.au/
- **Australian Taxation Office (ATO)**: Learn about taxation in Australia, including filing taxes and understanding the tax system. Website: https://www.ato.gov.au/
- **Department of Education, Skills and Employment**: Explore educational opportunities in Australia and access resources for students and job seekers. Website: https://www.dese.gov.au/

2. Immigrant Support Organizations

- **Settlement Services International (SSI)**: SSI provides support and services to refugees and migrants in Australia. Website: https://www.ssi.org.au/

- **Migrant and Refugee Women's Health Partnership**: This organization focuses on the health and well-being of migrant and refugee women. Website: https://mrwhp.org.au/
- **AMES Australia**: AMES offers a range of services to support newcomers in language, employment, and settlement. Website: https://www.ames.net.au/
- **Refugee Council of Australia**: An advocacy organization working to promote the rights of refugees and asylum seekers. Website: https://www.refugeecouncil.org.au/

3. Online Communities and Forums

- **Poms in Oz**: A forum for British expats living in Australia, offering advice, support, and a sense of community. Website: https://www.pomsinoz.com/
- **Expat Forum**: Connect with expats from around the world, including those living in Australia, to share experiences and tips. Website: https://www.expatforum.com/

4. Useful Apps

- **myGov**: Access various Australian government services and information in one place. Download: myGov on the App Store[1] | myGov on Google Play[2]
- **SBS Radio**: Stay updated with news, radio programs, and podcasts in multiple languages. Download: SBS Radio on the App Store[3] | SBS Radio on Google Play[4]
- **Medicare**: Access your Medicare information, find

---

1. https://apps.apple.com/au/app/mygov/id1003332447

2. https://play.google.com/store/apps/details?id=au.gov.dhs.mygov.android

3. https://apps.apple.com/au/app/sbs-radio/id504200399

4. https://play.google.com/store/apps/details?id=au.net.sbs.radio

healthcare providers, and submit claims. Download: Medicare on the App Store[5] | Medicare on Google Play[6]

5. Publications and Books

- **"The Australian Way: A Guide to the Good Life" by Michael Hyde**: A book that explores Australian culture, lifestyle, and social norms. Available on Amazon[7]
- **"The Little Book of Australia: A Snapshot of Who We Are" by David Dale**: A concise guide to Australian culture, history, and quirks. Available on Amazon[8]
- **"The Lucky Country: Australia in the Sixties" by Donald Horne**: An insightful book on Australian society and politics in the 1960s. Available on Amazon[9]

6. Educational Resources

- **TAFE Australia**: Explore vocational education and training courses in Australia offered by TAFE institutions. Website: https://www.tafeaustralia.edu.au/
- **Study in Australia**: Learn about studying in Australia, including courses, scholarships, and student visas. Website: https://www.studyinaustralia.gov.au/
- **IELTS (International English Language Testing System)**: Prepare for the IELTS exam, which is often required for visa applications and university admissions. Website: https://www.ielts.org/

---

5. https://apps.apple.com/au/app/express-plus-medicare/id869398897

6. https://play.google.com/store/apps/details?id=au.gov.dhs.medicare

7. https://www.amazon.com/Australian-Way-Guide-Good-Life/dp/0977544010

8. https://www.amazon.com/Little-Book-Australia-Snapshot-Who/dp/1740661662

9. https://www.amazon.com/Lucky-Country-Australia-Sixties/dp/1863958219

7. Government Settlement Services

- **Settlement Grants Program**: Australian government program providing support and services to help newcomers settle successfully. Website: https://www.homeaffairs.gov.au/about-us/our-portfolios/settlement-services
- **Newcomer Information and Support**: State and territory government websites offer valuable information and resources for newcomers, including settlement services and support. Find your state or territory's website[10]

Remember that the journey of settling in Australia is unique to each individual and family. Utilize these resources to navigate your path, and don't hesitate to seek assistance from government agencies and immigrant support organizations as needed. Your journey in Australia is filled with opportunities for growth, learning, and exploration, and we wish you all the best as you continue to make Australia your home.

---

10. https://www.australia.gov.au/information-and-services/immigration-and-visas/state-and-territory-government-websites

Printed in Great Britain
by Amazon

43211674R00067